UNDER PROMISE OVER DELIVER

UNDER PROMISE OVER DELIVER

How to Build the
Preeminent Law Firm
in Your Market

KEN HARDISON

Published by Advantage, Charleston, South Carolina.
Member of Advantage Media Group.

ADVANTAGE is a registered trademark and the Advantage colophon is a trademark of Advantage Media Group, Inc.

Printed in the United States of America.

ISBN: 978-1-59932-498-2
LCCN: 2014956742

This publication is designed to provide accurate and authoritative information in regard to the subject matter covered. It is sold with the understanding that the publisher is not engaged in rendering legal, accounting, or other professional services. If legal advice or other expert assistance is required, the services of a competent professional person should be sought.

TreeNeutral

Advantage Media Group is proud to be a part of the Tree Neutral® program. Tree Neutral offsets the number of trees consumed in the production and printing of this book by taking proactive steps such as planting trees in direct proportion to the number of trees used to print books. To learn more about Tree Neutral, please visit www.treeneutral.com. To learn more about Advantage's commitment to being a responsible steward of the environment, please visit www.advantagefamily.com/green

Advantage Media Group is a publisher of business, self-improvement, and professional development books and online learning. We help entrepreneurs, business leaders, and professionals share their Stories, Passion, and Knowledge to help others Learn & Grow. Do you have a manuscript or book idea that you would like us to consider for publishing? Please visit advantagefamily.com or call 1.866.775.1696.

TABLE OF CONTENTS

ACKNOWLEDGEMENTS

I want to thank all of those who helped me become the person who could write this book. The list of people I could thank would fill up another entire book, but let me mention a few who had the greatest influence on me. Cheryl Leone, for helping me to see the opportunities in life. Dave Favor, for his management mentorship in my early years of running a large law practice.

Dan Kennedy and Jay Abraham for expanding my marketing knowledge beyond what I ever imagined was possible. I want to especially thank Marilyn Beasley for all her dedication, support, and hard work during the bad times and good times in helping me build a Preeminent Law Firm. And finally, I want to share my sincere appreciation for the dedication, hard work, and creativity of my second family at PILMMA: Valerie, Billy, Nikki, Lori, and Simon.

INTRODUCTION

This book is going to hand you a shortcut to achieving the same success as a lawyer that I have achieved for myself. I started out the hard way, by trial and error, learning what it takes to build a successful law practice. Over the last 32 years, I've made many mistakes, some of which I share here. Eventually, I learned how to make it easier for myself to grow my personal injury law practice into one of the most successful firms in the state of North Carolina, before selling it to my partner and starting a new law firm in a neighboring state.

As well as running a busy Social Security Disability law practice in South Carolina, I am the founder and president of the Personal Injury Lawyers Marketing & Management Association (PILMMA), the only place for personal injury and disability lawyers to learn how to grow and better manage their practices.

From a young age, I was shown the importance of helping other people and I made this part of my daily life, first as a personal injury lawyer and secondly, by helping other lawyers to grow their own practices.

I learned the hard way about the strategy of preeminence and eventually put it into practice with my own law firm. I learned the value of being seen by people, especially clients and past clients, as their problem solver. As their helper. As their trusted legal advisor.

Preeminence is the strategy that will enable you to beat your competitors every time. By being the preeminent law practice, your firm will go further than any other to serve your clients and establish a reputation that attracts more clients.

Preeminence is about doing whatever it takes to be the best at what you do.

I define a successful law practice as one that practices the principle of preeminence and manages its staff and its marketing to ensure consistency exceeding your clients' expectations. A successful law practice is one that allows you to take off a month or two, while everything keeps chugging along like a well-oiled machine.

Of course, I wasn't always a successful lawyer. I started with very little and climbed my way to the top. In this book, I will share what you need to do to achieve the same success in building a preeminent law firm, and how to do it.

I was born December 23, 1956, in a little town called Dunn, North Carolina. My mother had an eighth-grade education, my father a fourth-grade education. My mother worked in a sewing factory and my father worked for a building supply company. I wouldn't say that we were poor, but we were definitely lower-middle class, a blue-collar family. I started working in tobacco fields when I was 10 years old. I did that job until I was about 14, when they started putting some kind of pesticides or herbicides on the crops that made me sick.

So, I got a job at a country grocery store bagging groceries, and that's where I learned how to be a butcher.

Carlie C. was a boss who was helpful and kind—a pillar of the community. I saw how by helping others he was respected in the community and made for himself a good reputation. Carlie C. cut me a break by letting me play football while I worked.

During high school, I worked 30 to 40 hours a week as a butcher and also was able to play football. I was a linebacker and the team captain. Between my junior and senior year, my father got a job offer in a town about an hour and a half away. I was dating a girl, Terry, who actually became my wife several years later. I did not want to move, and I talked my parents into letting me stay. I had already bought my own car, a Volkswagen that I paid $600 cash for. It was a straight-gear, a manual transmission car, and I didn't know how to drive one but I learned.

I rented a room for $15 a week from an elderly lady. Her son was the chemistry teacher at school. I was pretty much on my own when I was a senior in high school. My father said I could only return to live at home once, but that would be it. He was not going to offer any support, and I would be completely on my own.

My friend Joe helped me out. I had very little spare cash and Joe worked at Kentucky Fried Chicken (KFC). The rules were that any KFC chicken that wasn't sold at the end of the day was to be tossed in the garbage. Breaking company rules, Joe would leave a box full of chicken in the alley at the rear of the KFC at the end of the day. I would drive by and pick it up, and that would be my dinner.

I did what I had to do. It was about more than survival. I had the goal of graduating in mind, so I did what I had to do to achieve that goal.

I graduated from high school. I made pretty good grades and ended up in the honor society. I was still working, and even picked up a second job delivering newspapers on the weekends—300 of them every morning across a 60-mile route.

After graduation I continued to work, and I enrolled in a small school about 15 miles away called Campbell University. Initially, I went in as a trust management major. My girlfriend Terry was working full-time as a secretary at a local factory, and attending community college. She also babysat for a lawyer named Gerald Hayes. I used to go over after I got off of work and sit with her, and then I started talking to Gerald. I'd think, "He's helping people. He's his own boss and he must be getting paid pretty well because he has a nice house, a nice car, and nice clothes." Everybody seemed to like him. I thought that might be the life for me, because I wanted to be my own boss and start my own business. I knew that for sure. I didn't want to work for somebody else the rest of my life.

So I changed my major to pre-law government. I graduated and got into law school at Campbell, which was a new law school. I worked hard and made Law Review. And, by the way, I was never the smartest kid. I had to work for everything. But I was pretty good at structuring my days and working smart. Terry became my wife and she gave birth to our first child, Brad, on December 1, 1979, my first year of law school, right before exams. We had our second child, Jess, during the last semester of my third year, April 8, 1982. I had two kids, I was in law school, and I was working in the law school library.

I also started a business called Eastern Legal Research. For that endeavor, I placed an ad in the local law school paper, offering to do legal research for $15 an hour, and it went out to all of the lawyers in the state. I hired students to do the work and I paid them $8-$10 an hour, depending on how good they were.

I had a pretty good little thriving business, and my office equipment consisted basically of a Radio Shack answering machine connected to my home phone. I sold the business to another law student the year I graduated, and I was making a pretty good living between that and working in the law library maybe 10 hours a week.

During law school, I had clerked with different law firms—criminal, business, and personal injury—so I could figure out what kind of law I wanted to practice. I determined that I really liked doing consumer law, dealing with people and helping people, not businesses.

When I graduated, I went to work for a firm down in Beaufort, North Carolina, and moved my family down there, down to the beach. I was working 80-hour weeks in a big personal injury practice, every day including Sunday, but only Sunday afternoons, because I had to go to church in the morning and then to lunch.

I was about three or four months into the job when I asked if I could take off a Saturday. I'm a big UNC fan—North Carolina Tar Heels—and this was in 1982 when Lawrence Taylor was playing linebacker for them. I wanted to go see a game on a Saturday, so I asked the head of the firm for the day off because we didn't have any trials the following week. My friends had managed to get tickets to the Carolina Clemson football game. The game was a big deal. My boss said no.

I went back to my office and thought about it. I had always worked. I was always one of the best employees. I'd always given 120 percent, and this really made me mad. I had two kids and a wife at home and she wasn't working, and I thought to myself, "If I'm working this hard for this long and he won't let me take Saturday off this one time, then he'll never be happy with me and I'll never be happy working for him." So eventually I said, "Screw this."

I just went into his office and said, "I'm taking that day off, and by the way, I'm quitting." I said I'd work until he could find somebody to replace me, and then he started backpedaling. I said, "No, this is the way it is. I'm just going to do something else." This was the end of October, and I stayed until the middle of December.

I went back to my hometown and opened a solo practice with $2,500 that I had saved up. I wasn't even able to hire a full-time secretary. I hired a woman, Marilyn Beasley, for four hours a day and she's still with me today, more than 32 years later.

The first year of practice, I grossed $36,000 and netted maybe $16,000. There was a firm across the street that had been there since 1929. They started associating me on cases. I had gone around to every law firm in town and told them if they had any work they didn't want to do—tedious work, research, cases that they didn't want to deal with or whatever—I would take it. When I hired Marilyn, I was able to leave the office and go around to the country stores, and sit there and drink some bottled pop with the local businesspeople or farmers to see what was going on, trying to build a referral base. I was also on the court-appointed list.

Within two years, I was doing so much work for that firm across the street that they asked me to come in and be a partner. They did real estate, trusts and wills, some transactional work, and insurance defense. In a small town, you kind of do everything. I built up a personal injury practice and a little bit of a criminal practice over the next 12 years, basically without doing anything other than grassroots marketing. In those days, if you did anything other than put an ad in the Yellow Pages, you were deemed unprofessional. And if you put in a really big ad, something catchy other than just your name and your telephone number, you were called unprofessional.

So I did what was known as cross-selling. I sent letters to my clients and word got around. I grew the business every year for the next 10 years, until about 1994, but the early 1990s was when TV really started taking off with lawyers. In our TV market, there were several lawyers who just pounded the airwaves. In 1994, even though I was doing a really good job, getting better results for my clients and working many hours, our business kind of flattened. In 1995, it actually went down about 10 percent. I thought, "What the hell is going on?"

I started to examine the situation and I determined that it was due to TV advertising by our competitors. It really hit me in 1995, when I was still doing criminal law and one of my DWI clients came into the courthouse wearing a cast on his arm. I said, "What happened?" He said, "Oh man, I got hit by this truck. It T-boned me." I said, "Well, have you settled your case?" He said, "Oh, no. I hired a lawyer up in Raleigh, the guy on TV." I said "What? I do that kind of work." He said, "Yeah, but this is all they do and he's on TV."

It was sort of an "a-ha" moment. I don't remember the name of the law firm, but I remember that they were not good trial lawyers. I thought, "This is not fair that lawyers who are substandard are advertising and I'm doing a great job for my clients and they don't know any better." Back then, there was no rating system for consumers to consult. People just believed what they saw on TV.

So I went to my two partners and told them we needed to start advertising. I said, "I don't really like it, but we have to take action." All of the other lawyers in town were feeling the same thing. We would all be in a courthouse moaning and groaning and doing nothing about it. I told my partners that we needed to start marketing. I said, "I really don't know how, but I'm going to learn." They disagreed with me and we had a little standoff. So I left in September 1996, taking with me an associate and some files. It was an amicable breakup and we're still friends today.

I'm a voracious reader, and in 1996 I read a book called *The E-Myth* by Michael Gerber. It's about working on your business and not necessarily in your business, and about having systems. I didn't know anything about that. They didn't teach me anything about that in law school. I just knew this was a good book and it taught me that to really make big money, you've got to get people working for you, because there are only so many hours in a day and you can't do it all by yourself.

So I started reading every book I could get on marketing. I would go to marketing events for non-lawyers and try to grab some of their ideas and bring them back to the legal community. Of course, I had to worry about the ethics rules, because we do have to deal with that. But I just made it a mission and actually still do it to this day. I go to several seminars a year that have nothing to do with lawyers, just to see what's going on, to see if I can get an idea that I might be able to apply. If I remember correctly, banks came up with drive-thrus and then McDonald's had them next. Businesses have always stolen from other industries and applied the ideas to their own industries.

In 1997 or 1998, I went out and mortgaged everything I owned. I signed a note with the bank and put up my house. I got a half-million-dollar line of credit. I spent it all on marketing, and probably 80 percent of it went into TV ads. I must say, the cases did come in and we grew very fast. We went from two lawyers and three staff members in 1998 to 13 lawyers and 43 staff members in 2003. My income went up, and the gross went up about 1600 percent.

During that period I made a lot of mistakes. I had nobody in the legal field to tell me what to do. I had to go to non-legal industries and find things to apply to my practice. Some of it worked, and some of it didn't. I hired some really good people who were smarter than I was. We created processes, systems, procedures, mission statements, and core values. We set up the practice like a business, but still had that family atmosphere where we treated each client like they were the only client.

Basically, I'm an entrepreneur at heart. I love building things. But I also get bored. So in 2007, I started thinking about selling. I had to find the right person, and I did. His name was Ben Cochran. When the process was finalized, I went down to the beach to start the next chapter of my life. There were no marketing groups for injury lawyers back then, so I started a group called Lawyers Inner Circle. Basically, we'd get together two or three times a year and talk about what was working, and we'd show each other our ads, whether they were from TV, the Yellow Pages, or direct mail. We also talked about how to get referrals. There were maybe 10 or 12 of us in the group. This was the beginning of my Mastermind groups. Even though I didn't call it a Mastermind group, this is where I began Masterminding. Those early Masterminds had a huge impact on my practice and the other lawyers' practices who were members. All of our members flourished. But more about the power of Masterminds later.

In 2009, I had to change the name. Some organization called Lawyers Inner Advocates or Advocates Inner Circle said I was violating their trademark. I didn't really care, so I changed the name to PILMMA, which is the Personal Injury Lawyers Marketing & Management Association. This is where my passion is. This is what I really have fun doing—helping other lawyers—because I hadn't had that help myself. Now we have members from all over the country and we have some in Canada and Australia. I facilitate four different mastermind groups. I consult and coach members, lawyers, and firms all over the country to help them double their practices in less than 24 months. I've helped many of them grow their firms by 30 to 60 percent every year.

I have devoted the last 15 years to researching, studying and analyzing marketing and management for law firms. As a direct result of my above activities, I have authored several books covering the subject prior to this book.

Here is a list of some of my published books:

- Co-author: "Workers' Compensation: 'You Take (45 percent of My Breath Away,'" *Campbell Law Review*, Volume 4, p. 107, 1982
- Author, *How to Effectively Market Your Personal Injury Law Practice in the 21st Century*, 2009
- Co-Author, *Power Principles for Success*, 2010
- Co-Author, *How To Build Your Law Practice with a Book*, 2010
- Co-Author, *Protect and Defend*, 2012
- Co-Author, *Stand Apart—Stand Out Strategies From Today's Leading Entrepreneurs and Professionals to Help You Achieve Health, Wealth & Success*, 2013
- Author, *SSD: Ultimate Guide to Winning Your Social Security Claim*, 2013
- Co-Author, *Why Lawyers Fail to Convert New Callers into New Clients (And What to Do About It!)*, 2013
- Author, *How to Effectively Market Your Personal Injury Law Practice in the 21st Century*, 2nd edition, 2014

In the last four or five years, I've done a lot of consulting work. In this book, I've taken my experiences from building a law practice and helping other lawyers build their law practices, and without revealing names, share them with you in hopes that you will learn from them, enjoy them, and grow from them.

CHAPTER ONE

Why Aren't All Lawyers and Law Firms Equally Successful?

M ost lawyers are stuck. They are stuck in their businesses because they lack certain things. It varies depending on the lawyer and who you talk to, but over the years in my consulting work, I've found that the top seven things lacking are: motivation, talent, systems, leadership, urgency, vision, and capital.

MOTIVATION

Let's talk about lack of motivation. One of the first books I read when I was thinking about doing some marketing was *Think and Grow Rich* by Napoleon Hill. He says, "All limitations are the ones you put on yourself," and I agree. Lawyers are taught in law school to be analytical and very critical. We're trying to figure out ways to solve problems. What are the roadblocks or blind spots that keep us from doing what we need to do for our clients?

We're taught to be skeptical and always try to see why we can't do something. That is not good training for a businessperson or entrepreneur, because as an entrepreneur you want to figure out how to get over that obstacle—not just what the obstacle is. Where motivation is concerned, you need what I call "fire in the belly." You've got to be driven. You've got to have the mindset that the glass is half full. I've always said that there is no such thing as failure, just learning experiences. I think Thomas Edison said that, but I second it.

Some mistakes are more expensive than others, and I've had my share. I've made some $200,000 mistakes, some $10,000 mistakes, and some $2,000 mistakes. The key is to learn from them and not make them twice. That's one reason I love the masterminds, because you can eliminate those $200,000 mistakes by learning from the mistakes of others.

You can't give up and you've got to have perseverance. Chet Holmes says in his book *The Ultimate Sales Machine* that you need "pigheaded determination." You can't let obstacles get in your way; you've got to figure out how to get around all of them. And you've got to want it. When I interview a prospective new lawyer, I want to know if they had good grades in law school and all of that, but I really want to know more about what they did during their high school years. Did they work jobs? Did they work during the summers? Did they work after school? Did they come from a blue-collar family or white-collar family? I want to find out if they were motivated, and if they understand our client base, the blue-collar people.

I used to ask this question: "If you could work 40 hours a week and make $60,000, or you could work 60 hours a week and make

$100,000, which would you rather do?" That's a roundabout way of asking them if they're driven. What they did when they were in high school and how much they want to work now is more valuable to me than probably the rest of their resume and qualifications put together.

I want somebody who is motivated, because as John Morgan says, "You can't teach hungry." Something motivates everybody, but it's the degree of motivation that matters. I've read enough books and talked to enough experts to know that everybody has something that motivates them. For some people, money offers no motivation. For other people, it's all about money. For some people, it's about prestige. For others, it's about power. Some people want recognition. But when you find someone with that burning desire—that fire in their belly—hire them quickly! You want to hire people who have the strengths your firm needs. One mistake I made was to hire people because I liked them and they interviewed well. Another mistake that cost me money was that I hated to fire people. Today, my slogan is, "Hire slow, fire fast."

So the biggest mistake I made when I took a half-million-dollar loan out was that instead of holding back some of it for hiring staff and purchasing supplies and computers, I threw it all into marketing. I went six months without taking any money out of the firm. It was bad. I was 60 to 90 days behind on certain bills. I never missed a payroll check, but cash flow was horrible. It was terrible. And I had already spent my line of credit. That was a major mistake. It almost bankrupted me.

I survived it, though, and when it turned, it was ironic. I'll never forget it. It was June 1999. I thought, "If this thing doesn't change by the end of the year, I'm going to break it up, because I've been six months without a paycheck." My savings were pretty much depleted. It's the first time I ever got depressed in my life. But then it clicked and I had my first $100,000 month in June 1999, and it went wild after that. I've never had a month since that I haven't done six figures. I made it through, but man, I would never tell somebody to do it exactly the way I did it. That was probably the biggest mistake I've made in my life. I was very entrepreneurial and driven and wanting to succeed. But other than running a three-man law firm, I really didn't have any experience running a business. It's dangerous to give somebody with no business experience that kind of money.

TALENT

I used to think that if you worked hard and outworked your competition, you were going to succeed. I've always done that. In every job I've ever had, I was the guy who worked the longest hours. I always came in first and left last, whatever it took. I figured if I did that, and had great motivation, I was going to beat the competition. But sometimes you need to focus that motivation on working smarter, not just harder, and surrounding yourself with people who are smarter than you are in certain areas, and who compensate for your weaknesses. You can't be great at everything. You've got God-given talents, what I call "unique strengths." I'm a big idea guy. I'm very good at figuring out strategies and strategic planning, have a great mind for marketing, and I can come up with some great ideas.

When it comes to computers and software and technology, I'm terrible. I don't even know how to type. But I can hire people to do the things I'm not good at instead of trying to learn it all. They used to call Henry Ford the "smartest man in the world." One day a newspaper reporter asked him a bunch of questions, and Ford did not have answers for them. The reporter said, "Aren't you supposed to be the smartest man in the world?" Ford said, "On my desk, I have a phone. All I have to do is hit a button and I can have access to someone who knows these answers. Why do I need to know everything when I've got people I pay to know what I don't know?"

You can't be the master of everything. But a lot of lawyers' egos are so big that they cannot admit they have weaknesses, and they won't take advice from somebody else. They think they know it all. It's sad, but sooner or later they're going to fall, just like K-Mart did, just like Best Buy is going to do. You have to change. You have to surround yourself with people who are smarter than you, and your ego has to be able to handle it. Forget about working on your weaknesses. I say leverage your strengths and surround yourself with people who have strengths in areas where you have weaknesses. I think that's a key to a very successful business, whether it's a law firm or any other type of business.

This leads us to lack of talent. I've seen it over and over and over— lawyers who want to make all of the money and aren't willing to hire the best people because it costs too much. They're so cost conscious that they can't see the forest for the trees. They're shortsighted.

TESTING IS ONE OF THE KEYS TO PICKING THE RIGHT CANDIDATE TO FILL A POSITION.

I can't stress how important it is to your law firm's success to hire the right person for the right position. Testing is one of the keys to picking the right candidate to fill a position. I have been using Jay Henderson's testing and hiring program for the last 10 years, and I can confidently say that Jay has saved me hundreds of thousands of dollars during that time. Anyone can interview well. But Jay's test cannot be gamed or manipulated.

Preeminent Resource

Jay Henderson, founder of "HiringLawTalent. com," a unique hiring and management development service for lawyers who want to know exactly who to hire, what to expect, will they succeed, why they will succeed, what motivates them, how they learn, and how they perform best.

Website: www.HiringLawTalent.com

Phone: 877-863-7133

You want to hire the best, and then you want to give them the tools and the training and the support to make them the best they can be. It takes work, though. It takes time and effort to hire the best people, because, as you know, anybody can give a good interview. You've got to make sure that they get into your culture.

It's not just about talent. It's also about fitting into a culture and having the same vision and core values as your place of employment. Employees want to be part of something bigger. If their job is to just process paperwork, that gives them no feeling of ownership.

It's like Zappos. At an employee's six-month anniversary, they offer the employee $2,000 to leave, to not go on with them. Not only do their hires have to be smart, bright, talented, and manageable, but they also have to have the same mindset and have the same values as you and your law firm. They must buy into your mission statement and vision for your law firm. You are probably thinking your firm doesn't need a written mission statement, or values. You're thinking that is only for large corporations like Zappo's or General Motors. Well, you are wrong. You want to create a firm workplace culture. The only way to accomplish this is with a written set of values, a mission statement and a vision statement. My newest firm, Carolina Disability Lawyers LLC, only has five employees. We still have all of the above. Below are our values, mission, and vision statement.

OUR MISSION

Our mission is to give the best client service possible!

Our firm is based on a foundation of values and policies, which are binding for all attorneys and staff, and serve to guide us in everything we do. Our values are:

OUR VALUES

1. Dedication to Client Service
   Everything we do is for the betterment of the client. We don't just want to exceed expectations; we want to WOW our clients to the extent that they never stop talking about us.
2. Truth
   Our daily goal is to be truthful to our clients and to each other. This open truthful communication will lead to trust. Trust is the backbone of any relationship and we will strive daily to build trust and relationships with each other, our clients, and the public.

3. Learning

We will strive to be continual learners and stay abreast of new cutting-edge technology and new laws that will help our cause and our clients. We want to be creative and think outside the box in solving our clients' problems.

4. Genuine

We will be genuine with each other, the public and our clients. We will always strive to communicate using layman's terms when possible.

5. Compassion

We will treat our clients with compassion and empathy. We will always put ourselves in our client's shoes. We will treat each client the way we would treat our grandmother.

OUR VISION

We will be the leaders in Disability Law with a team of bright, highly motivated, compassionate people who are dedicated to helping the less fortunate and disabled. We will be the shining star example of a top-rated client service law firm other professionals firms will try to emulate. We will become the trusted legal advisor for all of our clients and everything we do will be for the betterment of our clients. We will build and nurture lasting relationships, with our clients and all others we meet and communicate with. Our firm shall be viewed as caring, compassionate, yet aggressive toward accomplishing our goals. Carolina Disability Lawyers will be the career choice for the brightest and most compassionate attorneys and staff in the field of Disability Law.

You need the above to help create your firm's work culture. What is "workplace culture?" Simply stated, a workplace culture consists of the shared values and behavioral norms that impact how your staff and attorneys interact with you, each other and your clients. A strong healthy workplace culture can really impact the performance of your employees and the performance of your law firm. A strong workplace culture can:

1. Provide a sense of identity
2. Generate a commitment to your firm's mission
3. Clarify and reinforce standards of behavior

Jay Henderson's test is perfect for determining if your new hire candidate will fit into your firm's work culture.

One time, I had to fire one of the hardest-working, most productive employees I ever had. Why? She was terrible with the clients. She was short with them; she was rude. So I counseled her. I said, "You produce at least 50 percent more work than any paralegal I've had. Why can't you be nice to our clients?" She said, "Well, when I'm at work, I'm busy. I don't have time for that stuff." I said, "Here's the deal, I want to keep you. You've got two choices. I'm either going to have to fire you, or I will pay for you to go to a course, a Dale Carnegie course, on How to Win Friends and Influence People." She said, "I'm not going to do it," and I fired her.

This is what I ask my lawyers (and I stole this from my friend John Morgan): "Whatever type of firm you've got, if your dad or mom or brother needed your law firm services, would you let your firm handle their case?" If you can't answer that question with "Yes," then you've got a problem. You'd think it'd be easy to say "Yes," but you have to really be honest about the answer. I'm probably not the best legal mind in my law firm, but I was a great negotiator and a fair trial lawyer. I was great with clients but I also wanted somebody in the firm that I would be willing to trust my family's life with in a courtroom. Or if my brother or my son needed to go get disability, I would let one of my people handle it because I had that much confidence in them. If you can't say that, then you've got a lack of talent in your firm.

SYSTEMS

Next is lack of systems. Like I told you, I had two "a-ha" moments in my life. One was with the criminal client of mine who hired the TV lawyer to help him with his personal injury case. The other was when I discovered systems.

SYSTEMS ARE VITAL. IF YOU CAN SYSTEMATIZE EVERYTHING, AND I MEAN EVERYTHING, YOU'VE GOT IT MADE.

I'm talking about client service, referrals, intakes, hiring and firing, taking time off of work, and how to handle a case from beginning to closing. We've got systems for everything—and all of those systems have processes and procedures.

I think it helps you become more streamlined and organized, but it also prevents you from becoming dependent on any one person. You don't ever want to get into a position where someone can hold you hostage. If you've got systems in place—procedures and training systems—you're in great shape. If you've got an employee who gets killed tomorrow, is it going to affect your business? Other than a little hiccup, is it going to be devastating to the running of your business? If it is, then you've got problems. You need to have systems, processes, and procedures. You also need to have a contingency plan for losing key employees.

Ninety percent of the time when people are not getting things done right, it's not their fault. Sometimes it is, but if you've done your job up front—screening people and hiring the right people and getting great talent—then it's usually your fault, because you either did not provide the tools to get the job done or you didn't provide the proper training. When mistakes are made, I usually go back and tweak my training or send them back to training and make sure they know what they're doing. If that doesn't work, it means the process needs adjusting.

As lawyers, we're supposed to be the big commanders-in-chief looking over battlefields. I imagine myself like that. But really, if it's all smoke-filled and you can't figure out what's going on, your frontline people know better than you do what needs to be done. So when I'm creating these systems, processes, and procedures, I get a lot of input from my staff. We've actually got forms and systems that allow them to provide input and tweak the systems, because there's always new technology coming out. There are new ways of doing things. Laws change. So it's a constant evolution. If you set it up and say this is the way we're going to do it, then forget about it, and five years later, haven't touched it, haven't adjusted for change—you're in for big problems. You're going to become a dinosaur.

It's a constant project, working with systems, processes, and procedures. You're always trying to improve them. We have a suggestion box at our office, and any time a person can make a suggestion of how to do something more economically, how to streamline something, or figures out a way to get more clients, they get points. At the end of the year, the ones with the most points get a week's paid vacation at a beach house. We encourage people to give us ideas. You need input from those who are intimate with the processes. That's what makes it all work. Don't kill the messenger. I see lawyers and managers who do that every time someone tries to share new ideas or different ways of doing things. If you knock down everything they say without even listening to it, they're going to quit coming to you with ideas. You can only go up against a brick wall so many times before you say, "Hell, I'm not going back. That hurts."

So that's why I think systems are so important, especially if you're doing any kind of volume. It's what I call working smarter instead of working harder. Putting in the work matters and putting it all in a system is key.

LEADERSHIP

Let's talk about lack of leadership. Everything starts at the top and runs down. If you've got a successful law firm and you look at the top dog, the leader, he's usually a great one. Everybody thinks a great leader has to be charismatic. Not true. Look at Tony Dungy, who used to be the head coach of the Indianapolis Colts. He was a quiet-mannered, soft-spoken man and he won a Super Bowl. Then you've got people who are very outspoken, and some of them can be like the Harbaugh brothers. One of them is a little more laid back, whereas the other one's a lot more outspoken about things. They're both great leaders. They both have very successful football teams. They achieve it in different ways, but they come from the same cloth.

When I practiced criminal law, there was this great prosecutor, the head prosecutor for a whole district. He was a hell of a trial lawyer. He was like a preacher. Fire and brimstone. He had control of the courtroom and he would shout and holler, but it was natural for him to do that. When he retired, an assistant prosecutor took over. He tried to emulate him and it just wasn't his style. He tried to act in a way that wasn't natural to him, that wasn't comfortable, and he was terrible at it. He was not in his own skin, and he was very ineffective. Finally, after about five years, either someone told him or he figured it out on his own, but he started being natural and winning cases and he got a lot better publicity. Don't try to be someone you're not! It will lead you and your firm nowhere.

You can be a great leader and not be a great manager. I think I'm a much better leader than I am a manager. I can manage, but I think my strength is in leadership. I try to surround myself with people who are better managers than I am to take care of the day-to-day running of the firm. I'm a deliberate type of person. But I'm sincere in it, and your staff and your lawyers know when you're sincere and when you're not. You've got to walk the walk and talk the talk.

You've also got to see the big picture. I learned a great lesson from a gentleman who was a retired IBM executive, Dave Favor. He came in and worked with me for four or five years. He told me, "You've got to make decisions based on what's in the best interests of the firm. That means it's not in the best interests of Joe, Katie, or even yourself. Now, most of the time, 90 percent of the time, you are the firm. So whatever that decision is, it's going to be aligned with you. But sometimes you might make a decision that's in the best interests of the firm that's not a good decision for you personally."

So every time I had a big decision of any kind I asked myself this question: What's in the best interests of the firm overall? Overall. And that's because I looked at the big picture. When you get bigger, you've got different divisions. You've got different people who have different interests and different agendas. But if you ask that big question and honestly answer it, you're going to make the right decision every time. It might not be the one that you really want to make, but it's going to be the best decision for the firm.

Sometimes decisions are hard. It's like coaching a football game. Sometimes you've got to sit the star player, and it's a hard decision. It doesn't matter which way it goes; the coach is going to get second-guessed the next day. I was watching a basketball game recently and Carmelo Anthony broke the scoring record for the new Madison Square Garden with 62 points. They took him out with seven minutes to go. The next day, a sportscaster said, "They should have left him in so he could have bumped it up even more." The guy being interviewed said, "What would have happened if he'd gotten hurt with two minutes to go? Would you feel the same?" The sportscaster said, "Well no, then I'd say the coach had made a mistake. He should have taken him out earlier."

IF YOU MAKE THE DECISION BASED ON WHAT'S IN THE BEST INTERESTS OF THE FIRM AND REALLY BE HONEST WITH YOURSELF, THEN YOU'RE GOING TO BE FINE. THAT IS WHAT I CALL GREAT LEADERSHIP.

It doesn't matter what you do; you'll always have people second-guessing you. The other thing is, you've got to be fair. I always say that I am a benevolent dictator. And what I mean by that is I've got the final say-so. I'm the one who put up all the money. I'm the one who almost had a mental breakdown because of it back in 1999. It is my firm and I'm going to operate the way I want. But the deal is that I've got to be fair to everybody. I always tell my people that I have high expectations of them and of myself. I'm firm, but I'm fair.

You've also got to be calm. When it looks like everything is falling to pieces, you've got to be like that little duck in the pond. It looks like it's just sitting there floating along the water. But under the water, those feet are going 100 miles an hour!

Just like that duck, you've got to project confidence, and be calm, cool, and collected. Everybody is looking at you as an example, and there will always be things that upset people. You've got to be the one who lays that wave of calmness over everybody and says, "It's going to be all right. Don't worry, this is how we're going to handle it."

Being a mentor is also important. When I built my first firm, I built it with younger lawyers and I did that on purpose. There are two ways to do it. You can either hire experienced lawyers who have proven track records, or you can hire people and mold them to be the way you want them. Either way is good, but I decided to go with younger lawyers whom I could mold. This way, they wouldn't pick up any bad habits.

I have found that when you hire lawyers from other firms, they come in and think they already know how to do everything. I'm not saying the way they do certain things is wrong. It just isn't my way.

I want everybody to sign the letters the same. I want all of the forms to be the same, and all of the procedures to be the same. I don't want 13 different mini law firms under one roof. I want everything to be congruent and streamlined, and everybody doing everything the same way, especially when it comes to sending correspondence out of the office. I want it all to look uniform.

YOU'VE GOT TO MENTOR PEOPLE AND INVEST IN THEM.

I've got four rules for when I hire somebody. First, I sit them down and go over what our expectations are. Next, I ask them what their expectations of us are, because we need to make sure that we're going to be able to fulfill their expectations. Third, I want to give them the proper tools. I want to give them the best chair to sit on. I want to give them the best computers and the best lighting. I want them to be aware that they've got the fastest computer and the best software available. I want to get them the best training. I'm investing in them. And fourth, I want to praise them in public and criticize them in private, because people like to be praised. For some people, that's their big motivation. We all like it. Nobody can tell me that they don't like somebody to pat them on the back and say, "Atta boy." I'm pretty confident in myself. I don't need somebody to tell me I'm good. But even I like being praised for a job well done. Everybody does.

THE WAY YOU TREAT YOUR STAFF IS THE WAY YOUR STAFF IS GOING TO TREAT YOUR CLIENTS.

It took me a while to understand this concept. But it is just this simple. When I first started, I was growing a big practice and paying my lawyers good money. I was investing in them and I felt like that's what they were supposed to do—a great job. I used to think, "Why the hell do I need to tell them they're doing a great job? That's what I'm paying them to do." Luckily, my office manager, Cheryl Leone, was a wise woman. She made rubber ink stamps for me to stamp on paralegals' work, like "Great job," or a smiley face. She made me stamp it on work they'd done because I had such a problem with telling people how great of a job they were doing.

But I got better at it over the years. It's still probably not one of my strengths, and I try to do it when I have meetings and other interactions with my employees. I acknowledge people in public on the good work they're doing. That's a sign of a good leader. It's not all about you. It's about seeing the big picture and investing in people. The way you treat your staff is the way your staff is going to treat your clients. So if you treat them with disrespect, cuss at them, and show them no empathy, then that's the way they're going to treat your clients. I've seen it.

I had to fire a lawyer one time. He was very active in the Academy of Trial Lawyers and he was a great trial lawyer. He was great with clients and got good verdicts. But he was the biggest procrastinator and just could not get work done and would not follow the systems—and this was a guy who I would have let represent my mother. Clients were complaining because he didn't file paperwork when he was supposed to, and things like that. I don't think he was lazy; I just think he got sidetracked a lot.

He was very much into client service, and he'd talk about strategy, so I told him, "You talk a great game and you've got game, but you just don't produce enough. And when you don't keep a case running down the road, that's poor client service and that doesn't meet with our core values, right?" We want to exceed people's expectations. We want to give them that "wow" experience. We want them to walk away from the experience willing to give us referrals even if we lose the case. We want them to know that we push cases. That is an attractive trait in a law firm.

So I had to fire that lawyer and that was the hardest firing I ever had to do because genuinely I loved the boy. He was a great lawyer. But, looking at the big picture, it was not in the best interest of the firm to keep him. We had all of these procedures in place to push, push, push. He just wasn't holding up his end of the bargain as a member of the firm. He wasn't following the system, and he wasn't giving good client service.

There is a saying: a legal case, most of the time, is not like fine wine; it doesn't get better with age. Sometimes there are exceptions, but overall, the case is not going to get better. In fact, it could get weaker, because people's memories fade. As a defense lawyer, I used to love to delay a criminal case for years and years, because people's memories fade, people get hurt, people die, or people get transferred. That's what the insurance companies want to do, too. They want to delay, delay, delay. And if you let them do it, what they're doing is winning and that doesn't go with our core values. It's poor client service.

It goes back to being a good leader. It wasn't fair to the other lawyers in the firm to keep him on. So I had to let him go. To this day, I admire him. I think he's a great lawyer. That was a tough decision and one that helped me further realize that being a leader is having to make those tough decisions. I lost sleep over that one because it kept conflicting with the other idea of mine, which is: I want great talent. But you've got to see the big picture, and that's part of being a leader.

URGENCY

Let's move on to urgency. A lot of lawyers are the biggest procrastinators in the world, last-minute people. I don't know if it's because they're so busy or what it is. But they procrastinate as much as, or worse than, anyone I've ever seen. If you don't instill a sense of urgency in your firm to get things done, no one else will. It starts with leadership. It starts at the top. Here's a good analogy, and I did not make this one up, but I love it. I tell my people, "I want you to make believe that there's a person who's got a gun to your mother's head and if you don't get this done by tomorrow noon, they're going to blow her head off. Does that make it clear how urgent this is, that I want this done?"

That's why you set benchmarks. I set benchmarks for very important cases. You always need to be setting the bar higher and higher, because you always want to be better today than you were yesterday, and better tomorrow than you were today. So you've got to instill that concept in your people. When a person gets released from an auto accident, I want to have his medical records in-house within 45 days. I have reports that my people have to fill out, and they have to say when the medical records were obtained. We've got all of this on a case-management system. I actually run reports on each lawyer and each staff person who is overdue. You're going to have some people who are overdue, but if it goes above the norm, then I want to know why.

That's all part of instilling a sense of urgency. You're setting deadlines and telling people that what they are working on is urgent.

Once they get the records in, I add another deadline. I want to have the demand package, or the brochure to the insurance adjuster, out within 30 days after that. And we run reports on that, too. Then, after that gets sent out, I want the case settled or a lawsuit filed within 90 days, so there's even more urgency that I am instilling in my people.

As I said before, a legal case is not like a fine wine. Pushing things through is good client service and it goes with our core values. It becomes important to people. If it's not important to you, then it's not going to be important to them. You can't manage what you can't measure. So I try to measure all of these things and instill urgency. I've been to law firms where files are just sitting, collecting dust, and clients are groaning because nothing's getting done on their cases. The head of that firm might say, "I've got cash flow problems," but I would reply, "Yes, but you're sitting on a gold mine." You need to instill some urgency in your firm, and it starts with you.

One time our system got bottlenecked. We had more cases than we could get out in a certain part of the month. I called for a Saturday workday and paid everybody extra and called it a brochure-out party. I brought in pizza, and every time we got a brochure done, we'd hit a bell. You can make it where it doesn't have to be like a job. You can make it fun if you think about it, but at the same time you're instill-ing that sense of urgency that says, "We've got to get this work out."

There are a lot of lawyers sitting on gold mines if they'd just dig them out. But they're too complacent and there's no sense of urgency about them. They don't have that drive and determination. The work is just not getting done. The lawyers who instill that sense of urgency are the ones who are very successful. The ones who get things done, and who make sure their staff gets things done, are the most success-ful. You either get a team of people who will commit to get it done or you get rid of them. This is where talent, motivation and leadership create a perfect storm of success.

VISION

Now, about vision. You've got to know where you want to go and where you want to end up. You want to know where you want to be and where your firm wants to be in one year, three years, five years, and even ten years. If you don't know, how can you convey to your team where you want the firm to go? There's a tool that can help you with organizing your vision and bringing it to fruition. Cheryl Leone with Catalyst Group has developed a "Triangle for Success." A template is set out on the next page. Basicially, you pick three goals you want to achieve personally and professionally at certain ages in your life.

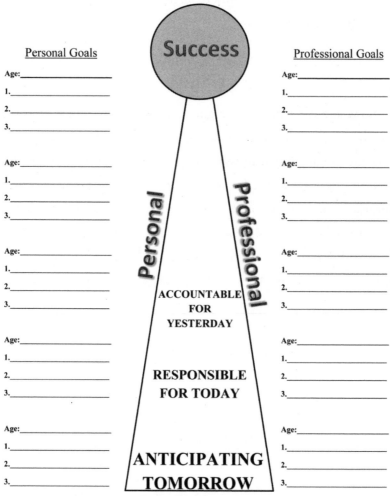

Personal Goals

Age:_____

1._____

2._____

3._____

Age:_____

1._____

2._____

3._____

Age:_____

1._____

2._____

3._____

Age:_____

1._____

2._____

3._____

Age:_____

1._____

2._____

3._____

Professional Goals

Age:_____

1._____

2._____

3._____

Age:_____

1._____

2._____

3._____

Age:_____

1._____

2._____

3._____

Age:_____

1._____

2._____

3._____

Age:_____

1._____

2._____

3._____

Success

Personal　*Professional*

ACCOUNTABLE FOR YESTERDAY

RESPONSIBLE FOR TODAY

ANTICIPATING TOMORROW

You control your future, your destiny. What you think about comes about. By recording your dreams and goals on paper, you set in motion the process of becoming the person you most want to be.

Henry Mason

You put your professional goals on one side (and they can be your firm's goals), and you put your personal goals on the other side. You can update the goals year by year or even every five years. Where do you want to be? Right now I'm 57. Where do I want to be when I'm 60, professionally? Where do I want to be personally? Where do I want to be when I'm—65? 70? 75? Where do I want my firm to be in those years? The best part is, you can change your mind every year. That's having the vision, the foresight. You've got to have goals to know where you're going.

It can change. It does change. You might change the entire direction of the firm. Something might happen that changes it all. But if you don't know where you want to go, how are you going to let everybody else know? I like to have monthly meetings with the lawyers and the staff separately. We go over the vision for the firm, and make sure we're all focused on the same goals.

At the beginning of the year, we have a "vision day" where I close down the firm and rent out a hotel conference room and bring all of my employees in to talk about the goals we've met in previous years. We recognize those efforts and go over human resources issues, like 401(k) and health insurance, and get everybody up to speed. We also talk about people's successes and the firm's successes. We give out several awards, including one for the person who had the most ideas implemented from the suggestion box. Then we talk about where we're going this year—our "big, hairy, audacious goals"—the one or two or three things that we're really going to be pushing the coming year.

Such a goal might be that you want to go paperless by the end of the year. You might want to streamline the intake systems. Whatever it is, you've got to convey to everybody that these goals are important to you as a leader and also important to the firm. Maybe you are opening a new office in a new territory: "The goal is to have a manned office in Hoboken, New Jersey, within 18 months, and this is our game plan." It's as simple as that. But it needs to be done; it needs to be communicated clearly. You want everybody to be on the same page and know what's going on. I've seen other firms where people don't know what's going on and they're literally the last to know. That makes them feel like they're not part of the team and they question their worth. You want them to feel a sense of ownership. You want them to take part in things and take ownership, and be part of the growth, part of the vision. You want them to grab ahold of it and share it with you.

You want them to feel like they are part of something bigger. You want to build a culture in your firm that everyone is important to the firm's success. You want to instill ownership of your firm's goals, values, and vision. You want everyone on board. Your appeal should sound something like this: "Now we can go help people in Hoboken, New Jersey, and give them the same great services we've given to people in Newark. So we're going to spread the word. We're going to go out there and help these people and dominate this market, and you're part of it. I want you to be on the bandwagon with me, and I'm looking for input. Put it in the suggestion box or set up a meeting with your manager. Bring it to us, because we're looking for ideas on how we can go into this market and succeed. We're also looking for ideas on how we can streamline the paperless initiative. We want to go green."

Whatever your goal is, you want to convey it and you want buy-in from your employees. This shows them that you value them, which you should. If you don't, you've got problems. At the end of every year, I review the employee manual and make any needed changes to it. I get everybody to read it and then we all go over the changes that were made, and the reasoning behind the changes. Maybe a change was made because of a suggestion from a staff person and it's something that gives them extra benefits. Maybe the change takes something away from them. Whatever it is, we always explain the reasoning behind it because you can cram stuff down people's throats and say, "This is the way it is now," but it's better to tell them *why* this is the way it is now. It's always a good idea to explain your decisions. When you explain why you're doing something, your employees don't have to agree with it, but at least they'll know where you're coming from.

One year, we went from paying all of the cost of insurance for employees to paying 75 percent of it. I had run the numbers and created a graph and showed it to the employees. They got to see the numbers trending up anywhere from 15 to 30 percent a year. I said, "The bottom line is, we've got two choices. You guys can help pay your insurance premiums, or we can do away with it altogether. I don't think you want to do away with it. So this is the deal. You're going to have to contribute 25 percent." And I presented them with research that showed how many other local firms either didn't offer insurance at all or made their people pay 50 percent of the premiums. So I settled the matter, but I also gave them reasons for my decision—reasons they could understand and appreciate. I didn't just say, "This is the way it is now." I told them why.

BRING EVERYBODY IN AND MAKE THEM FEEL LIKE THEY'RE PART OF SOMETHING BIGGER.

Again, I always go over our core values and what we stand for, along with our mission statement, when we're reviewing or adjusting the manual. Just bringing everybody in and making them feel like they're part of something bigger is how you start to build a successful law firm. I really feel strongly about this and I make sure to always follow these procedures to a T.

Core values are non-negotiable. When you determine your core values, you've got to say, "This is a 'non-negotiable' to me. We're going to give exceptional client service, and it's non-negotiable." That's why I fired that woman who completed 50 percent more work than anybody else I'd ever had in my firm—because she didn't give exceptional client service. We want to give exceptional client service because that gets us referrals. Could I have made more money off of this employee? Maybe in the short term, yes, but I had to look at the big picture, which is part of being a leader.

How much do referrals cost you, folks? Nothing. Where do my best cases come from? Referrals. I talk to other law firms about it all the time. The best firms' biggest moneymakers come from referrals. They don't come from advertisements; they come from referrals. They come from past, satisfied, happy, raving fans and clients. So exceptional client service resulting in referrals is a non-negotiable for me. It might not be for some firms. If it's not, that's fine. But you've got to stand for something, right? If you don't stand for something you stand for nothing. Live it, breathe it, eat it, sleep it. I think your partners and your lawyers have got to do that, too, or it won't last.

Some lawyers say, "Oh, that's just a bunch of hogwash. I don't have time for that. That's all theoretical. That's MBA material." I'm telling you, I've done it from day one and it does make a difference. And if you look at the very successful firms, they've got core values, too. They've got them spelled out and they drill them in, and they preach them. It's proven to be effective. Look at other very successful companies, like Zappos, IBM, even Coca-Cola. They all have very specific core values. A lot of law firms don't have a strong sense of their core values, and I know it's hindering their success.

CAPITAL

Let's talk about capital. One of the biggest problems a lot of law firms have is that they're short on capital. They just don't have the money to do what they need to do. You can do a lot of things that don't cost money, but if you want to really grow, and maintain a seven-figure law firm, or a mid-eight-figure law firm or more, you've got to have money. That's just the way it is. Whether you start from scratch or you've already got a firm, whether you've got plenty of money or you have to obtain a line of credit, you need to manage your finances wisely.

Either you've got to have capital or you've got to borrow it. Banks will not really loan money to contingency firms, because they don't have anything they can go in and repossesses other than equipment that is probably worth ten cents on the dollar. So usually when you're dealing with a bank, you've got to put up something other than your business. You could put up real estate or CDs, or your savings. Or you could get somebody to sign with you, somebody who is worth millions. You've got to put up some kind of collateral, because most banks, especially in this climate, will not loan you money based on your income sheet or your inventory of cases, because they can't go get those cases off the shelf and auction them off at a fire sale if they need to.

So that's a big challenge. On the other hand, in recent years there are now companies that will loan money to lawyers because they understand the business. They have people who can look at your inventory of cases and your cash flow and understand how it all fits into the legal market. They will loan you money, but it's not cheap. You will probably have to pay 30 to 50 percent more in interest than you would from a bank. But if you can't get the money from a bank, it really doesn't matter, does it? Think about it. You have to have money. You either need to have it already, or borrow it.

ALWAYS KEEP A LINE OF CREDIT JUST IN CASE YOU HAVE A BAD MONTH.

You should always have a line of credit so you can use it when you have bad months, because even when you've got a good, reputable, solid law firm, you're going to have ups and downs. I always keep a line of credit just in case I have a bad month. My old partner believes in holding back two or three months of overhead in cash reserves. That's a great way to operate if you can afford it, because you're actually making money on your money and you've got a cushion if you have a bad month. We can't always control our income the way a firm that bills hourly can. They know if a lawyer bills 200 hours a month at $200 an hour, the payment is due the 10th day of the following month, and the money will be there. Not so with personal injury and disability law firms.

We are contingency-based firms and we never know when the money's going to come in, because we have no control over whether a person is going to get better, or when an insurance company is going to pay the money that is being sought. That sometimes puts us in a cash-flow quandary. Successful law firms do one of two things: they borrow money or they save up until they have enough. The bottom line is, it takes money to build a successful law firm. It takes good people working for you, and it takes systems and clients and all of that. But, first and foremost, it takes money.

CHAPTER TWO

Creating the Infrastructure

Why is creating an infrastructure in your law firm so important? People always come to me for help in growing their practices, and their most common question is, "How can I get more cases?" They want me to give them strategies for obtaining more cases. I always say, "Are you ready for more cases? Do you have the infrastructure?" Without a solid infrastructure, you're heading for disaster. You've got to be able to handle the influx of business. A good example is the recent Obamacare launch. They did a good job of informing the public and proposing it. When the launch date hit and people were supposed to be able to go online and sign up, the government website didn't have the infrastructure in place to handle all the business coming to it. The website crashed.

It's the same with a law firm or any other type of business. If you do not have the proper infrastructure set up, you'll end up offering bad client service. You won't be able to handle your cases properly and your clients are going to fire you. Even worse than firing you, they'll post negative reviews on Yelp and Google. That can really destroy your practice. You need to have the infrastructure in place to handle the workload you want. Otherwise, you are setting yourself up for massive failure.

Infrastructure is made up of systems, processes, and procedures that allow you to properly handle the work you obtain and give great client service with quality legal work. That's how you create a preeminent law firm, by having the proper infrastructure in place. You have to be able to deliver when someone picks up the phone and wants to hire you.

PROCESSES

You need systems for hiring people, firing people, and providing client service, among other things. Any task in your firm can be systematized with a process. Even training can be systematized. I hear a lot of lawyers say, "Oh, I just don't have time." You must take the time. It's like building. If I were to build a $10 million house and I didn't want to take the time to put in a proper foundation, it would be a piece of junk that would crumble to pieces. It's the same with a law firm. Infrastructure is a key element. You have to build a solid foundation.

HOW DO YOU BUILD INFRASTRUCTURE? IT'S LIKE EATING AN ELEPHANT. YOU DO IT ONE BITE AT A TIME.

A process can be as simple as figuring out everything you've got to do to get from point A to point B. Get your staff involved. Take the hiring process for example. What are the steps, and what are the forms that you use? Who are the people involved in the process? I can look at the form I use and say, "Step one: Who's responsible? Step two: Who's responsible? Step three: Who's responsible?" Say it's a 12-step process and your staff looks at it and says, "I think we can knock this down to nine steps. We really are duplicating ourselves here." Well, you've just streamlined your infrastructure and probably saved yourself some money, too.

It's good to involve your frontliners, the people who actually know what is going on in your law firm, perhaps even more than you do. They know the details. Once you end up streamlining with their help, it will become an evolving process. Things will change. You can always come back and ask for feedback from your staff or from whoever is in charge of a particular process. "How can we make this better, smoother, easier, more streamlined, more effective?" It's a process. You do it one bite at a time. You get the system down and do it the same way every time, until you adjust it, and then you do it that way every time. Once we hire someone, following our step-by-step process, we have an orientation process. It's just little things like showing them where the bathroom is, getting them to read the policy manual and sign off on it, and giving them their keys and their parking pass. Make sure you have a checklist and you can say, "People know how to do that," for each task that needs to be done.

It used to be that people would stay with a company forever. But now, probably 80 percent of your people will not be with you for more than three or four years. If you have the proper processes in place, if they leave or become ill, or can't work for some reason, you can just slot somebody else in. It's so much easier to keep the machine moving down the road when you don't have disruptions.

Don't forget about training manuals—the "how to do it." You must have processes and procedures. A process is not the same as a procedure. A process defines *what* needs to be done and which roles are involved. A procedure defines *how* to do a task and usually applies to a single role only.

If you say, "This is a lot of work," well, quite frankly, it is. But if you're trying to build a preeminent law firm, you want the best of everything, and it takes time to build the best. You just start at the beginning and do it. It's a process in and of itself. It takes time. But the rewards are great if you take the time to invest in it. Think of it as investing in your future, your firm's future, your staff and your own peace of mind. It's going to make life and running the firm so much easier for you. I promise you will be grateful you did. It's a lot of work on the front end, but it makes things easier down the road.

At my old firm, we had manuals and processes and checklists for everything. I even had a client policy manual in which we talked about our mission, our core values, what we stood for, what we stood against, and how we wanted to treat our clients. We actually gave our employees a 10 question test on it, and they had to get at least 80 percent of it right. If they missed one of the questions I thought was really key, I would ask them to go back over the manual and retake the test. If you don't make it important to you, it's not going to be important to them. So, right at the outset, we let the people we hire know that client service is the number-one priority in our firm. To build a preeminent law firm, client service has to be your number-one priority.

TO BUILD A PREEMINENT LAW FIRM, CLIENT SERVICE HAS TO BE
YOUR NUMBER-ONE PRIORITY.

REFERRALS

You get your best cases from referrals, and you get referrals from people who know they can trust you. These are the people you've already done a great job for. I call them "raving fans." People don't refer bad cases to you. They refer cases that are good because they want you to like them and be grateful for their referrals. Your work starts with these systems and processes, even though you wouldn't think that client service and obtaining referrals would have anything to do with systems. It does. You've also got to have marketing systems. If you set up a whole marketing plan, then you have to have a system for implementing it.

We've actually created a system to promote our consumer educational books on TV. You can get the books for free, and then there's our consumer education process, where a potential client can call in and leave his name and address. Once that happens, the name gets e-mailed to another person who has a form letter or template to complete. We send the caller the book, plus some other free information. The whole system is set up to create what I call the marketing funnel. Systems are not just for infrastructure but for marketing, too. We'll discuss this later but the point is that systems are very important. They help you manage your law firm.

IF YOU CAN'T MEASURE IT, YOU CAN'T MANAGE IT.

If you've got all of these systems, checklists, processes, and procedures set up, you can run reports and set benchmarks. If you don't know your metrics—and by metrics I mean what people are doing and what stages your cases are in—then you can't manage your law firm, especially as you grow. If you want to grow your small or mid-sized law firm into a large firm, you are going to have to have the systems, processes, procedures, and checklists in place. If you don't, you're going to have chaos.

CODING

Take coding, for example. We code every case. It's either a new case or we give it initials that act as codes for "recovering," "released," "brochure-ready," "brochure out," "file suit," or "in suit." That's important, because we can look at where each case is in the process, and then we can determine somebody's caseload. We can predict what their workload will be like in the near future and what kind of new cases they can take on. It helps us to manage our cases, so that we're not overloading one lawyer or one case manager. Even though somebody might have more cases, the workload should be equal, depending on where their cases are in the system.

With coding, you can actually manage each case. We have processes and procedures where when a person gets released from a doctor, he goes into the case management system and gets tagged. Depending on the type of case, they've got 30 to 45 days to submit all of their medical records to us. If they don't, a red flag comes up. I can create a report and say, "Let me see all of the cases in which the person has been released and it has been more than 45 days and the medical record is not in." Then I can run that by the lawyer. I can run that by the case manager, and then I can see if there's some kind of trend. If somebody has 80 percent of their cases in that kind of shape, then I've got a problem. I've got to go in and dig deeper and find out what's going on. It might be a good reason or it might be a really bad reason, but you don't know which it is if you don't have the infrastructure, the processes, and procedures set up to determine that.

Once the medical records are in, another checklist pops up and they have 30 days to get the demand (or what I call the brochure) out to the insurance company. Then when we're ready to run a report, we can run it daily, or weekly. We can run it according to the total number of cases, or in relation to one lawyer or a single case, and you can see how many people are not getting their brochures out in 30 days. I've got Jane over there, who has 20 percent of her cases not getting out on time. I've got Joe over here, who is at 80 percent. I've got a problem with Joe. I have to see what's going on. These benchmarks, case management tools, processes, procedures, and checklists all help you manage your firm more effectively. They let you know what your metrics are. It's not just about how much money is coming in and how much a case settled for. It's really about managing the workflow with benchmarks.

KNOW THY NUMBERS.

KEY PERFORMANCE INDICATORS (KPI)

Now let's talk about what I call Key Performance Indicators (KPI). They are essential to building a preeminent law firm and they should be monitored weekly, bi-weekly, or monthly, depending on what they are measuring. Let's say I want to know how much a case is costing me, because I want to know my return on investment (ROI). If a client acquisition costs me $300 via the Internet, or $800 via a TV ad, I want to know what kind of case each one is. For an SSD case, I know that I don't want to pay much more than $300 or $400 dollars to attract a client. But if I'm taking on a nursing home case, I could pay $2,000 to $3,000 a case and still enjoy a nice return on investment. The key determiner would be what the average fee is. The larger the average fee, the more you can pay to attract a case.

Say you want an 8-to-1 return on investment and your average fee on a nursing home case is $120,000. You would divide $120,000 by 8, which would yield you $15,000. You would then know that you can spend up to $15,000 per case. Your next step would be to determine what your cost per lead is and what your conversion rate is. For example, based on the last two years of historical data, you would know that you actually sign up only one out of every ten people who contact you. This is a 10 percent conversion. Thus, you would know that you can spend a total of $15,000 for ten leads. Another way to look at it is, you could pay $1,500 per lead. If you wanted a 10-to-1 ROI, then the numbers would be different using the same formula.

This table illustrates ROI:

Average Fee	$120,000
Divided by ROI	8
Cost per Case	$15,000
Cost per Case	$15,000
Conversion Rate	.10
Cost per Lead	$1,500

Let's use SSD cases for our next example. My average fee is $3,000, and my minimum ROI is 8-to-1. My conversion rate is 24 percent, as shown in the table below:

Average Fee	$3,000.00
ROI – divide by	8
Cost per Case	$375
Cost per Case	$375
Conversion Rate	.24
Cost per Lead	$90

In this case, I can pay up to $90 per lead. The point is, what you can pay per lead depends on several factors: (1) average fee, (2) your desired ROI, and (3) your conversion rate. Once you determine these three variables, you can then calculate out how much you can spend per lead to get the cases you want.

Of course, all of this assumes that you know your numbers. Sadly, the majority of lawyers don't. If you want to be successful and make money, then you must know your numbers. To do less is to depend on luck.

Most lawyers don't think this way. They bunch everything together and say, "Well, this is what my average fee is." They don't even know what their average fee is. They think they do, but they don't. They say, "This is what it costs me to do the case." They don't look at a case to see if it's a good business decision.

PAY ATTENTION TO THE NUMBER OF CASES YOU
SIGN UP EACH MONTH.

Another Key Performance Indicator to pay attention to is the number of cases you sign up each month. When you know that, you can also look at how many calls you're getting per month, and what your conversion rate is. If you're getting 400 calls a month and signing up only 50 cases, that's a 12.5 percent conversation rate. That's not very good. You should try to figure out why that rate is so low.

If I use the appropriate software, I can easily see that Julie is signing up 40 percent, but Joe is signing up only 5 percent. In that example, I would have a problem with Joe. What's going on with him? I want to listen to Joe and see what's he's doing, or not doing. By looking at these KPIs, I'm not going to get all of the answers, but I'm going to see where I need to dig a little deeper and go behind the reports and find out what's going on in my firm.

I like to know how many cases are being closed. Am I closing more than I'm bringing in? If I want to grow, I need to sign up more than I close. If I'm closing 50 cases a month and only signing up 30 per month, I have to recognize that I'm trending in the wrong direction. If I'm closing 50 cases a month and signing up 100 per month, then I'm moving in the right direction and looking at pretty rapid growth.

You have to examine these things and try to go deeper and figure out why things are the way they are at that point. Sometimes the reasons are good, and sometimes they're bad. But you don't know what you don't know, and if you don't have these Key Performance Indicators in place, and the proper infrastructure set up, then you're never going to create a preeminent law firm.

LEAD SOURCES

Another Key Performance Indicator is the source of leads. If I know that TV cases are costing me $1,200, and that most of my TV cases are Social Security cases, that's not good. If they were worker's comp cases, then that would be okay. I can spend up to $1,500 on a worker's comp case. Find out where you're getting the best bang for your buck. You can't put all of your eggs in one basket. You might do TV advertising and some Internet advertising, and maybe some other things, too, such as guerrilla marketing, which we'll talk about later. But if you don't know what your marketing and advertising is doing for you, then you can't make intelligent decisions.

You have to weigh everything and look at the big picture and say, "I know I could just do all Internet, but I need TV, too. It helps my brand to be recognized on the Internet. Therefore, although I can't pinpoint it, I know that when I'm off TV, my Internet leads go down." I've actually seen this happen—a lawyer's Internet leads go down 10 or 20 percent if he stops advertising on TV. He may still be doing well but there's no way to quantitatively measure it, specifically, scientifically. He's just looking at trends.

For ROI, the rule of thumb is, you want at least eight times the return on your investment, and if you can get ten times, that's great. I've seen people get 15 to 20 times their ROI, which is super. It's important to calculate your ROI, because then you know where you're getting the best bang for your buck.

There are software products that can help you keep tabs on your Key Performance Indicators. What you want is a "dashboard" specific to your firm, and there's nothing out there that's really made to interface with your case management, because they don't allow APIs (Application Program Interfaces). Of all of the case management systems available, 90 percent don't have an API, so they won't connect to dashboard software programs. I've seen successful law firms hire people to create their own dashboards. They pull the information from Quickbooks, their case management systems, their intake software, and their phone systems. They pull it all together and they get real live dashboards. There are no dashboard software products on the market that are built specifically for law firms, so custom software is really the only way to go. I know of some law firms that have hired specialists and spent six figures on their dashboards. But you can certainly do it for much less than that.

The below figure is a screen shot from a preeminent law firm willing to share how one section of their dashboard works.

The figure represents an attorney's individual caseload report. By running this report, we can see how each attorney's caseload is positioned in the firm's process of handling a case. We can also see how productive each attorney is. With this one report, we can manage 50 lawyers more effectively than we could manage one lawyer without the report.

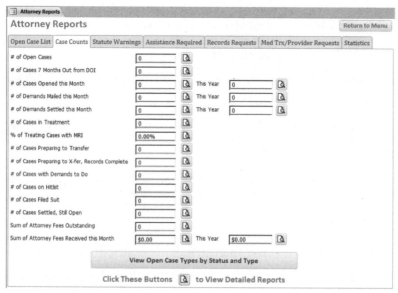

GAME PLANS

Part of creating your infrastructure is being able to see the end first. What I mean by that is, you've got to know where you're going or where you're trying to get to. What's the end game? That's what I always ask lawyers: "What's your endgame? If you could forget about money, forget about obstacles, in an ideal world, where do you see your firm and yourself in five years, three years, one year?" You've got to answer those questions so that you can create a plan to get there. I always say that a goal without a plan is just a dream. So write these things down. Create a game plan.

A GOAL WITHOUT A PLAN IS JUST A DREAM.

You need to create a business plan, a marketing plan, a strategic plan. What I like to do is set my goals. I know this year, looking at my reports, I'm signing up 100 cases a month. Next year, I want to sign up 125 a month. That's the growth I want. So that's my plan for next year, and I know that in three years I'll want to be at 200, and in five years I'll want to be at 300, or whatever that number might be. Whatever you want and realistically think you can do, that's what you should aim for. And you should create a strategic plan for how you're going to get there. After that, you've got to figure out a marketing plan that will help you meet your goals.

That's why all of these reports above, and the Key Performance Indicators, are so important. If you don't know where you are, how do you know where you're going? How are you going to get there? This historical data is very important. You might notice that in the last two years your average fee for auto accident cases has gone down significantly. You need to look at this data and see where it's trending. You might also notice that your worker's comp fees are going up; why is that? Dig in and figure out why.

Think of an airplane pilot and what he must do. Any time he flies, he must file a flight plan and follow it so that he doesn't crash into other planes that are also in the air. It helps him get from point A to point B, which is his goal. Without that plan, the odds of him running into another airplane greatly increase. The same concept applies to a ship captain. If he's in New York and he wants to get to England, he can't just go out and start sailing. If he doesn't chart his course, how will he ever get there?

Lawyers get so busy working *in* the business that they don't work *on* the business. You've got to take time, at least five to ten hours a week, to work *on* your business. And when I say, "work on your business," I mean, "stay away from dealing with cases." Work on marketing and management, look at your reports, and look at all Key Performance Indicators.

Without a plan, you're going to be all over the place. The best way to work on your business is to chart where you want to go. I like to work backwards. Say I want to get to 125 cases per month. I look at the trends—my historical data from the last two years, or the last year. I look at what's working and what's not working. I make a budget and a marketing plan that show how I'm going to get these cases, and I allocate my budget for these types of marketing tactics, and then I work backward from there. Say that next year one of my goals is to go paperless. I say, "Okay, this is how we're going to do it," and then I work backward by quarter, then by month, then by week. If you really want to get sophisticated, you can work backward by day. I delegate work to the people I want to do the tasks at hand,

and then I hold them accountable for getting those things done with deadlines.

IF YOU WANT TO BUILD A PREEMINENT LAW FIRM AND BE SUC-CESSFUL, YOU MUST TO DO WHAT 90 PERCENT OF THE LAWYERS ARE NOT DOING: CREATE A PLAN.

I'm not saying that any of this is easy. Creating a plan takes work. But if you want to build a preeminent law firm and be successful, you've got to do what 90 percent of the lawyers are not doing. If you want to be in the top 10 percent of your peers, these are the things you must do. The hardest part is following through. Lawyers create all of these great plans and start out the first of the year with everybody onboard, going, "Rah-rah." Then people get busy, or something unexpected happens, and then everyone starts reacting instead of being proactive. People lose focus, and the leader or managing partner loses focus and doesn't hold people accountable. Or people come up with excuses and the leader lets them slide, and the whole plan goes to hell.

My uncle once told me, "Son, you're so busy working that you can't make any money." What he meant was, I was so busy working in my business that I could not work on my business and help it grow. If you're too busy doing cases or putting out fires and you can't get focused on growing the practice and holding people accountable to get things done, you're in trouble. You're on a treadmill. People will give you a thousand excuses about why they can't get something done, or what's wrong with it. Sometimes they're right—about 5 percent of the time. Ninety-five percent of the time, they're just making excuses. People will do no more than what you hold them accountable for. That's human nature.

SOLUTIONS, NOT PROBLEMS

When people tell me, "We can't get this done because of a problem," I respond, "When you tell me you can't get something done because of a problem, I want you to bring me two solutions." We've got to get their brains to start figuring out ways to solve problems. I don't want people coming in and saying, "We can't." I want them to say, "We're having problems getting this done, but here are a couple of possible solutions that I think might get us over the hump." That's the kind of people I want working for me. This is the mindset and accountability you want if you're going to build a preeminent firm.

Is it easy to find these people? No. But that goes back to my "hire slow and fire fast" philosophy. I would rather suffer and do without somebody for two or three months than hire the wrong person, because in the long run, I am still going to come out better. I know it. In my 32 years of experience, I've seen it. I've done it. I've made the mistake of reacting and saying, "Well, Joe is leaving. I've got to find somebody to replace him fast." I'd put out an ad and have somebody in there in a week just because I wanted to fill that position. It's like there was a hole in my bucket and I wanted to patch it up. What I was doing was putting a piece of bubble gum over it. It was just a temporary fix!

But that's not the way you want to do it. You don't want to put a piece of bubble gum over that hole. That's just a short-term solution, a reactive solution. You want to drain the water and get a welder to put the bucket back together and then you want to fill it back up again, properly.

ACCOUNTABILITY

A lot of lawyers, especially partners, have no one to hold them accountable. That's why I think having a mentor or a coach, or being involved in a mastermind group, is extremely valuable. In a mastermind group, you're there with like-minded lawyers and you tell them what your goals are and then you have to come back and face them. That holds you accountable and that's a good thing. We all need accountability to some degree.

YOU'VE GOT TO HAVE PEOPLE WHO ARE NOT SCARED TO COME TO YOU AND TELL YOU HOW YOU'RE WRONG, AND HOW YOU NEED TO RETHINK CERTAIN THINGS.

Lawyers have egos and pride just like everybody else, and they are more likely to get things done if they have somebody holding them accountable. It's hard to find people in your firm to do that, because you are in a position of authority above them. That's bad because you don't want a lot of "yes" people. To build a preeminent law firm, you've got to have people who are not scared to come up to you and tell you how you're wrong, and how you need to rethink certain things. That's how you're going to grow. I don't care who you are. You don't know it all, and they sometimes know more about what's going on than you do.

Preeminent Resource

PILMMA's Mastermind Group is where you'll get time where the entire group is focused on your law firm, your marketing, your challenges, and your ideas. The Mastermind Group is one of the most powerful business growth factors you can have.

Website: www.pilmma.org/mastermind

Phone: 800-497-1890

This is where a lot of lawyers miss the boat, and a lot of my mastermind members in PILMMA are very successful because they don't miss this boat. They get things done because they know they have to return and face everybody. We get them to commit and say, "I'm going to have this done by the next meeting," which is four months away. They might not have it completely done, but they're usually at least showing progress. It holds them accountable. If you've got a coach or a mentor, somebody to whom you have to answer, that's a great thing. I think we all ought to have somebody who will hold us accountable. I coach lawyers. I have coaches who hold me accountable, and I pay them a lot of money to do so. It's worth it. I have someone saying, "You need to get this done." It breeds success. That's something that most lawyers don't think about. They are successful or somewhat successful as far as they are concerned. They went to law school, they passed the bar, they have a law firm, and they think they already know it all, which is dangerous.

PARTNER VISION

You have to work well with your coach or mentor, and you also have to work well with your law partner if you have one. You must have common goals. Let's say one of you wants really high growth and the other simply wants steady growth. You're going to have a problem. You have to know where each person is coming from. You can do this by doing partner retreats. I recommend this at least once a year, where the partners hire a facilitator and go offsite to talk about growth and the future of the firm. You take the time to make sure that everybody is on the same page. Then, when you go back to the firm, you have a united front. There must be open communication, and when there isn't, firms break up. People hold things in. They build and build, and all of a sudden they explode. This happens most often in big firms. They are making loads of money, and then all of a sudden they break up.

It's hard to hold a firm together and build something that's going to stand the test of time if you don't have people with the same goals and the same vision. I started a Social Security practice in South Carolina in early 2013, and it's doing very well. I know that one of my weaknesses is managing it, and I don't want to manage it. So I advertised for somebody to come in and manage it for me, and I plan to make him a partner if everything goes well. I want to sort of "date" that person for about a year or two, and if it goes well, then I want to "get married." Partnerships are like marriages. So I hired Jay Henderson to test all of us. First, I got about twelve candidates and after I interviewed eight, I had three people I was interested in. Then I had them take a test, and this is the same type of test that I've taken.

Jay administered the test and when someone was not a match, he said, "This guy has got to go. He's not going to be good for you." So it got down to two people. Both of them were really good. Jay said, "Here's the key. You need somebody who you're going to be able to get along with, who's going to share your philosophy. He doesn't have to be just like you, but you must have enough qualities that are alike. In other words, the core values must be the same. You must also have the same vision."

So Jay looked at my test and the other two guys' tests, and he said "Both of these guys will work, but candidate A is going to cause you stress because you're opposites. You're always going to be clashing. Although you will be successful, it will be a stressful success. With this other guy, your core values and his core values align. He's much better at managing than you are, and you're probably going to be a lot better growing the firm with marketing than he is."

I said, "Well, that's what I want." That was the process I went through. I'm looking for a partner and I went through this whole process because I know what it's like to go through a firm breakup. I've been through two of them in the last 32 years. One of them went smoothly and one of them was like World War III. It's no fun. It's disruptive and it's stressful. It's not something you want to go through. It's like going through a divorce. Nobody wins. Nobody is happy.

So with my potential manager who could become my partner, my next step is to bring him in for a talk. If I can work out the financials, I'm going to hire him, whereas 20 years ago I would have just interviewed him, and if I liked the way he sounded and we hit it off, I would have hired him. I've learned a lot about hiring since then. You can't beat life's experiences as a great teacher.

What I've seen is that partnerships break up for two main reasons. One, you could be making a lot of money but if somebody feels like he's contributing more toward it and doesn't understand what you're contributing, sooner or later, he's going to get greedy and want more money. He will think he deserves more. The other main reason is control. It's like I tell people, "You can't have too many chiefs and not enough Indians." When it comes down to it, somebody must make a decision. What I've found is that my lawyers, my staff, and my team members just want to hear a decision. It goes back to good leadership. People just want a decision made, and even if it's a bad decision, at least they have something to go with. But floundering around and fluctuating back and forth, or stalling, or saying we're going to take it out for review and talk about it, is never good. You're going to lose enthusiasm, especially if you are reviewing it for two or three months. You're going to lose the respect of your people. They get tired of that and they will leave you.

If you're going to be a partner, then you or your partner must make a decision. I've seen firms with loads of partners. They have to put everything in front of a committee and nothing gets done. It's like working for the federal government. Everything gets caught up in red tape. The more successful firms make somebody a managing partner and let him or her handle the decisions. Let them run things and empower them. If they screw up, replace them. But you have to give them a chance. You can't micro-manage them with committees. I've seen firms that require a committee meeting to decide what temperature to keep the office at. That's stupid. Ridiculous. Talk about red tape! It's crazy.

CHAPTER THREE

Three Core Divisions of Marketing Your Law Firm

If you don't have the cases, how can you build a law firm? You have to figure out how to get cases, and you do that by marketing. Marketing is not the same thing as advertising. Marketing is the overall strategic plan of what your message is and what you want to project. Marketing is like the wheel on a bicycle, and advertising, in different mediums, is the spokes of the wheel. Advertising mediums include TV, radio, Internet, and referral systems, among others.

If you think about it, there are really three core divisions of marketing your law firm. One of them is "before representation." That's usually what everybody thinks about. It's finding, identifying, educating, and motivating people to hire your law firm for the first time. That's getting leads. But there are actually two other components of marketing your law firm—one of them is "during representation." If you can deliver the experience of exceptional client service as it relates to the strategy of preeminence, which I will discuss later in the book, then you can create raving fans who will give you great reviews and send you referrals and become repeat clients.

We don't have a lot of that in the injury and disability sector, but I have had people who originally got hurt on the job, and then five years later came back to us because they got into a car wreck, and then ten years later came back to us because they had become disabled. One client had moved out of town and still had my business card from 10 years prior. I did such a great job for him, and he had received such great client service, that he kept my card. He drove two hours to hire us, and he showed me that business card. It was ragged and torn at the edges. But he had kept it because I had become his trusted legal advisor. That told me something right there. That made me realize that it's not just about getting clients in the door. It's what you do after you get them in the door that can get you repeat business.

WHAT YOU DO AFTER YOU GET CLIENTS IN THE DOOR IS WHAT PROMPTS REPEAT BUSINESS.

The third core division of marketing your law firm is "after representation," and this is where most lawyers don't do anything. You want to nurture lifetime relationships with people who already know you and trust you. I've always said, "People hire lawyers who they know, like and trust." Lawyers often spend a lot of money trying to attract people who don't know anything about them, and they forget about the people they already know—the people they have already represented. These are the people who know them, like them, trust them, and hopefully are happy with them. Why not put your efforts on marketing to those people?

You don't have to prove anything to those people. All you need to do is let them know that you're still out there so that they don't forget about you. The key is to generate referrals from these people and get repeat business. I've found that 90 percent of lawyers focus on only the first stage. There is another 8 percent who focus on the first two stages. But very few, I'd say less than 2 percent, focus on all three. The lawyers who do this are the super-successful lawyers. They understand what it takes to be a preeminent law firm in their market, and they're working all three stages all the time.

PEOPLE HIRE LAWYERS THEY KNOW, LIKE AND TRUST.

You can't be all things to all people, and you've got to figure out who your ideal client is. If you look at your numbers, you will probably see that 80 percent of your fees are coming from 20 percent of your clients. Ask yourself, "What types of cases are giving me my biggest average fees?" You might find that you're getting your biggest fees from trucking accidents or motorcycle accidents—or maybe from worker's compensation cases in certain states. Whatever it is, you want to figure out who your ideal client is. Look at the demographics. What ages are they? Where do they work? What do they watch on TV? Which radio stations do they listen to? Once you figure those things out, you've got to figure out how to get those people to know you, like you, and trust you.

CHAPTER FOUR

Before Representation

Before representation, you've got to figure out how to get people to know, like, and trust you if they don't already know you. Figure out what kind of marketing tactics, or what kind of advertising, you are going to use to get people to pick up the phone and call you or inquire about your services. How are you going to get them to turn their heads in your direction amidst all of the clutter out there? People are getting a minimum of 3,000 marketing messages a day. So how are you going to get them to know you and like you—and ultimately trust you?

Branding is one way. It's really good for a company like Coca-Cola, which has an unlimited budget to spend. They can just bombard the market with their name, logo, and image. Most lawyers don't have that kind of budget for branding. What I've seen over the years is more direct response advertising, which isn't just, "Hey, we're here for you if you need us." It's more like, "If you have been in a car wreck, hire the tough lawyers." Or, "Tell them you mean business," or, "Call us now! Time is running out."

You've seen commercials that say, "You may be entitled to compensation. Call now! Act quickly!" This is direct response advertising. It's a call to action. When it's on TV, it's airing enough for it to actually be branding while it's also spreading direct-response messages. It's like a billboard with the Coca-Cola name and swoosh, and red and white colors, which is branding. But it's also a message directed straight at the consumer to make them take action.

TV MARKETING

TV has always been the number-one way to get people to know you and know your message. Radio is another one. Internet. Press releases. Direct mail. Pay-per-click. Newsletters. Mobile marketing. Billboards. All of these types of media are what lawyers use to get people they don't really know to understand what the firm stands for, why a consumer should hire them, and why that consumer should pick up the phone and call or e-mail them right now.

It all costs money. TV has been the king, and probably still is, but it's not as effective as it once was. Now, the Internet is number two, and it's overtaking TV. It used to be that the Yellow Pages were the way to go. Now, Yellow Pages are all but dead. I used to spend $650,000 dollars annually on Yellow Pages ads, and I did the tracking to find out how much each case cost me. In the early 1990s, it was $400 dollars per case, and then it went up to more than $2,000 per case by about 2005. Furthermore, a lot of these were not good cases, because people who use the Yellow Pages were calling lawyer after lawyer until they found somebody who would take their case. So I was one of the first law firms to pull completely out of the Yellow Pages in 2006. I was spending $650,000 and I think last year we spent $12,000. We took that money and put it into TV and Internet and got a lot bigger bang for our buck. And what I've been seeing in the last five years is that the cost per case for TV is also going up. There used to be three TV stations, or four. Now there are 300 to 500 cable TV networks, which means a huge fragmentation of the market. Also, there are a lot more lawyers advertising on TV than there used to be. In 2004, lawyers spent $250 million on TV ads. In 2008, that number grew to more than $500 million. In 2013, lawyers spent more than $700 million.

There are only so many injury cases, or disability, cases out there. The TV market is getting saturated. Ten years ago, lawyers probably spent $2 million in the entire Raleigh-Durham TV market. Now it's more than $6 million. In 10 years, the number of ads, or the amount of money spent on TV, has tripled. Another factor is that cars are being made safer, so people are not getting hurt as badly, which is a good thing. But for injury lawyers, it's a bad thing. If you take the saturation of the TV market and the increased spending by lawyers, and combine those two things with the fact that cars are safer, you've got a trifecta. The end result is the steadily increasing cost per case for TV advertising (see figure on next page).

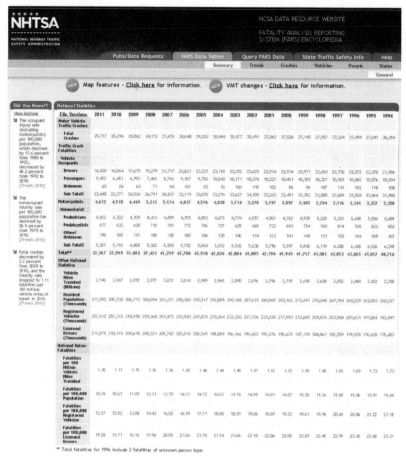

INTERNET MARKETING

I think TV will always be important, but I think the Internet is becoming more and more important. It's like the Yellow Pages. Anybody under 30 now doesn't even know what a Yellow Pages book is. They go directly to their iPhone, Google, or Yelp, or they just go directly to Siri and ask her. Things are changing and evolving, and lawyers must change with it. More than 52 percent of Internet searches are made with an Android or iPhone.

What does that mean? That means that everything is going in that direction, and people are paying attention to what other people are saying about you via social media. Yelp and Google use this approach. Siri searches use it, too. There are also other review sites. Things are changing—and the smart lawyers are changing too.

I think mobile marketing is now where the Internet was 15 years ago, when people were using desktop computers. They went from desktops to laptops. Now they're using iPads and other tablets. The iPhone is utilized by a more upper-crust clientele, as far as demographics are concerned. Androids are used more by the middle and lower socioeconomic classes. This is a big, big part of the market, and that is the market that lawyers doing injury and disability law are going after. I see that as a major area in which to market your practice. You want people to interact with you, and you want to educate them.

Also, think about your website. Everybody now goes to your website even if they see you on TV, even if they are holding your business card in their hand. I'd say 80 percent of the people interested in your services go to your website and check you out. What a great place to educate people. You can have your books there as well in a downloadable format. You can provide your free reports, your videos, and your general message through your website. That's a great way for them to get to see you, connect with you, come to know you, like you, and trust you.

We use Consultwebs. They do our online marketing, but we also still do a lot of in-house videos and put them on YouTube. So, we do some of our website on our own and we bring in help when needed.

Here's a big tip: When you put your videos on YouTube, you can include your URL in the description. But also, if you want to add some juice—what I call SEO juice—to your video, you can also provide the transcription. YouTube offers the technology to automatically transcribe your video for closed captions but it's not very accurate. So what I do is hire somebody to actually transcribe the video, and then I put that in the YouTube video description myself. The transcription will include the relevant keywords in there so that when the crawlers are going across those keywords, they are going to rank your video higher. Once someone has found your video on YouTube, a call-to-action in the video itself or the link in the description can drive traffic onto your website, where you can then convert them into leads and clients. Little tricks like that go a long way.

Preeminent Resource

Dale Tincher, founder of Consultwebs, heads up a team of web marketing consultants who deliver cost-effective and successful results for law firms across the nation. I have been using Dale and his team for over 13 years. They underpromise and overdeliver!

Website: www.consultwebs.com

Phone: 800-872-6590

Videos serve so many purposes. You can use them for SEO. You can use them to build a relationship and let people get to know you. You can use them to educate and build trust. You can use them to feature case studies, in which you actually talk about a client. You can also get the client to join the video and talk about how great you were. You're already educating them, but then you're building that relationship, too. The third thing, which is even better, is that people see somebody they can relate to. "This person likes me, or this person loves the firm, and they look like they're about the same socio-economic background as I am." They're thinking this in the back of their minds, and that's another connection.

One thing I did recently was take 25 frequently asked questions and put them, along with answers, on our website. For two months, I got my intake staff to write down questions every time somebody called with one. A lot of times, people call and they don't want to hire you right then but they want to ask a question. We also compiled all of our web inquiries to find the 25 most commonly asked questions. So we made a list of them and put them on our website.

Then I took it a step further. Instead of just answering them in simple text, I took each question and made a video for it to create what is called "long-tail phrases" that you see on web searches. People will execute a search and my YouTube video will show up, and that will send them to my website. I already know what people want to know, so I'm educating them. I'm getting SEO juice and I'm getting prospects to my website without actually having to pay a pay-per-click program.

PUBLICITY

The next thing is publicity, and this is not as much about direct response as it is about branding and getting your name out there. It tells the world that you're not all about the money. You could incorporate nonprofit causes into your publicity campaign. We're involved in the Helmets for Kids program, we sponsor scholarships, and we participate in distracted driving prevention programs for teens—all kinds of feel-good, worthy causes. It helps when people see these things on your website and other marketing pieces. They see that you're human and that it's not all about money for you. Lawyers, especially injury lawyers, have a bad reputation of being greedy ambulance chasers. Associating yourself with a nonprofit cause is a good way to show that you care about your fellow man, and not just the almighty dollar. People begin to like you and trust you, and know that you're doing things for the community and supporting good causes.

If you do this because you are genuinely interested, it will work. I tell lawyers not to get involved with nonprofit causes in which they have no interest. Find some causes that you like and get involved. Everyone has a cause or issue that has touched their family. We all know someone who has been through something. Find the cause that deals with that and support it. Make it personal. Do something that in some small way might advance a cure for cancer, or AIDs, or whatever cause hits close to home with you. But don't do it just to do it. If it's not genuine, it will show. When you go to events that you're simply sponsoring and putting the money up for it, the other people there will see right through you. Pick something that you really have a connection with.

The Susan G. Komen Race for the Cure is a great one. You could sponsor that. I've seen law firms get all of their staff members together and actually do the walk. Helmets for Kids is the brainchild of a lawyer down in Savannah, Georgia, who has been really successful with this. He buys bicycle helmets for kids and puts a little sticker on the back of the helmet that says it was donated by him. He created his own foundation. He's got an interest in it. He runs ads and he has collaborated with the police so that now all local police officers have these helmets in their cars, and if they see a kid riding a bike or a skateboard without a helmet on, they give the kid a helmet. The great thing about this is, the public perceives this law firm as being endorsed by the police.

We support this charity. What better way to get publicity and show that you can be trusted? The kids go home and say, "The police stopped me and gave me this helmet," and then the parents look at the back of the helmet and it's got, "Compliments of Hardison and Cochran" on it. How is that going to make that person feel? And then if they see us on TV or on the Internet, that helmet reinforces the fact that we can be trusted, that we're good people, and that we're a good law firm. They're going to like and trust you if you do things like this. They're going to want to go look you up on your website or more importantly, call your office.

We see a lot of kids, especially in high school, getting killed because they're texting and driving, so one of our other campaigns focuses on this issue. We give out bracelets that say, "Don't text and drive." You do that first step. You go talk to school groups and share some case studies of people you have represented, people who have been killed by somebody who was texting and driving, and you talk about how it affected their families. Or maybe you get one of your clients or ex-clients to talk to the kids about how a texting and driving incident affected them and their family. Maybe you can get someone who was actually doing the texting and driving and caused a big accident that hurt other people. These stories register with kids, and it makes your firm look good, look human to provide the opportunity for the kids to hear those stories. But again, you have to believe in it yourself, or people will see right through you.

EDUCATION-BASED MARKETING

Let's talk about education-based marketing. One of the ways to build trust with people is to educate them and let them know that you are the authority on a certain subject. And remember that people are different than they were 20 years ago. Back then, people went to a lawyer, listened to him, and did whatever he said. Today, people can look up anything on their phones. With today's technology, consumers are a lot savvier, a lot more educated, and they're looking for answers. They crave knowledge. To get them to trust you, instead of just trying to sell your services and be a purveyor of legal services, you need to educate them. By showing your knowledge, and helping them increase their knowledge, you're building that relationship and that trust. At the same time, you're building your authority in their heads. You will have them thinking, "This lawyer knows what he's talking about."

Writing short books is a great education-based marketing tactic. They don't have to be treatises. In fact, I tell lawyers to write their books at about a fifth-grade reading level and not make them too long. Number one, you're here to educate people, and number two, you're becoming the authority figure and the go-to lawyer on that topic. You're not writing to make yourself known as a "writer," and you don't have to write forever. Just establish yourself as an expert, cover the material as thoroughly as you need to, and wrap things up.

If writing is not your thing, you can talk your book through Adam Witty's publishing company, Advantage Media Group. I am actually using Advantage to write this book.

Preeminent Resource

Adam Witty, Founder of Advantage Media Group, helps busy professionals create, Publish, and Market a book to grow their business.

Website: www.advantagefamily.com

Phone: 866-775-1696

You can accomplish a lot of things with education-based marketing. People do not like to be *sold* to. They love to buy and they love to make decisions, but they don't like pushy people trying to sell them something. They get that all the time. They're just tired of it. It turns them off. So what you've got to do is create that relationship, and you do that through education. You build that. They get to know you, they get to like you, and they start to trust you.

Another marketing tactic is free reports, and these are great. You can make them downloadable on your website, and you can do it with pay-per-click advertisements. I've actually done it with direct mail for auto accidents. I've had people call me up and say, "Your report about how the adjusters do what they do and what was going to happen... it's like you're a fortune teller. You knew exactly what they were going to say, and what they were going to do, and if you know that much, I want to hire you."

When people have been in a car wreck, or they're going through a divorce or some other difficult experience, they want to be put at ease. They've got enough stress going on in their lives already, and they just want to have confidence in their legal advisor. By providing this report, you're creating all of the things that I've mentioned above. You're creating trust. They're beginning to like you and know you, especially if you put some real stories in your reports or your book, about how you've helped other people in similar situations.

Another way to do this is to speak at club meetings and nonprofit organization events. We used to speak at an organization that had an educational course for motorcyclists. It was a safety course for bikers who had gotten into accidents. It taught motorcyclists how to give medical treatment until an ambulance arrived, and most of it was EMT training. But there was more. They wanted a lawyer to speak about the Good Samaritan Rule. We also talked about insurance, about the uninsured and the underinsured, and things like that.

We bought them pizza for lunch. It was an all-day course on Saturdays, and one of our lawyers would do a one-hour presentation. We would give them a book about how to buy insurance in North Carolina, and we would give them a book about motorcycle accidents and safety, a book we produced at the firm. It was a consumer book, about 45 to 50 pages long. About two weeks after the first event we participated in, we received a call from a woman who had been hit, T-boned by a drunk driver at an intersection. Of course, I can't disclose all of the facts, but it was a policy limits case, and it was more than minimum limits. So we started doing that presentation every month. And then once we got the people into the presentation, we got them into our database. If we had their email we put them on our e-zine list. If we had their addresses, we put them on our newsletter list.

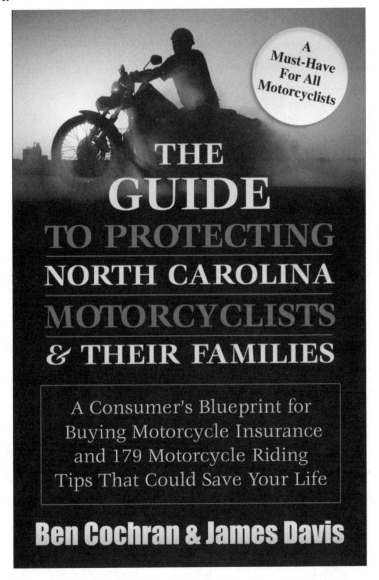

If you go to a Rotary club or any other civic club meeting, you can talk about buying insurance. You can talk about other legal subjects. You can hand out your book, which establishes you as the authority.

Clubs and organizations want to hear if you do Social Security work. You might consider talking to groups concerned with disabilities or diseases, such as lupus, diabetes, or multiple sclerosis. You speak to these groups and you tell them what the law can do for them. When you do that, you're educating them and giving them information. You never talk about the possibility of them hiring you. You're just building a relationship while educating them.

Hopefully, you can get them on your mailing list, and then you can keep educating them with different information that you send out during the year.

REFERRAL SYSTEMS

Most lawyers love referrals because they cost little if nothing to acquire. We all know most of our best cases come from referrals. People usually don't refer bad cases. The key is that most lawyers don't know: (1) where to go to ask for referrals, and (2) how to ask for referrals without really asking for them.

Think about where your ideal client will be going immediately before they would need your services. For example, somebody in a car wreck is going to need a wrecker service. They're going to use a body shop. They're going to be seeing an ER doctor. These are the key people who you want to know you, like you, and trust you. If you want to concentrate on dog-bite cases, who would you rather get to know than the local dog catcher, or animal control officer? Do you get the idea?

For a Social Security case, where would people be going if they were disabled? Vocational rehab. Or how about a pain management clinic? Divorce lawyers should get to know marriage counselors. Marriage counselors are there to try to make things better, but after a while, some couples say, "Hey, we need to get a divorce." Motorcycles? I want to get to know the leaders of the hog chapters, the motorcycle dealership owners, and the associations. I think you get my gist. Of course, you also want to meet other lawyers who don't practice your type of law.

THE KEY TO ALL OF THIS: CREATING REFERRAL RELATIONSHIPS.

When you go to these key people, don't say, "I want referrals." That is rude, crass, and ineffective. Here's a saying I got from Zig Ziglar: "You can get what you want if you help people get what they want." So I go to them and say, "What can I do to help you?"

For body shops, I might go in and say, "Hey, have you ever had problems with insurance companies? I'm here to help you pro bono, and I've created this book on how to handle your property damage claims in North Carolina. I'm going to put it out here free for all of your customers, and if they have any problems, even if I'm not representing them, give me a call. I'll help. Because I like you and I want to help your business."

What does that do? That creates a feeling of indebtedness, which flows from the doctrine of reciprocity. People are going to want to help you. Now, 50 percent of the time it's not going to work. You've got takers and you've got givers, and some people are only takers. But 50 percent or more of people will be appreciative, and the next thing they're going to say is, "What can I do for *you?*"

Of course, what you can do for me is refer me my ideal client. But you've got to go in there and offer help, sincerely, and you've got to go in there knowing that they might not do anything for you for a year or two. But if you set it up that way, instead of just going to people and being a taker, you're setting yourself up for potential success. Don't just take. And don't expect to get referrals without giving something first. If you follow this advice, I think you'll be a lot more successful with your referral systems. It's all about getting people to know you, like you, and trust you.

I don't refer clients to other lawyers unless I know they're going to do an excellent job and give those clients the same level of client service that we have given them. I say, "My only caveat is, you've got to give them good client service because that's what my people expect. If you don't do that, I'll quit sending people to you." I had a lawyer who was doing stock fraud cases back around 2003. He was a great lawyer. It was back when everything went to hell—Enron and all that stuff—and a lot of people got taken.

This lawyer was great. But I had a couple of clients call me after I referred them to him. They said he wasn't calling them back, and he was rude. I had one client who called me in tears about how rude he was to her. She told me exactly what he had said. I just picked up the phone and called him.

I called. "Is this true what Lilia said?"

He said, "I'm just busy. I've got more than I can do."

I said, "Remember what I told you?"

He said, "No."

"I told you that I can send you all the business you can handle, but that you have to give my referrals great client service."

And, of course, he was stressed. "I'm doing the best I can."

I said, "Well, listen. I'm going to have to quit sending you cases, buddy. And I hate it." I never sent him a referral again.

A SIMPLE THANK YOU

People like to be acknowledged for their referrals. If I send you a client and you're happy, maybe the next time you see me you should say thank you. Maybe I don't see you for a year or more. I don't hear anything from you. Or maybe I send you three and don't hear anything from you. I'm going to quit sending you people, because I think, "Well, number one, either the cases are not good cases, or number two, he doesn't really care one way or another if I send him clients. He doesn't appreciate my efforts."

I actually handwrite a thank-you note to everybody who refers me cases, whether it's a lawyer or an insurance adjuster or someone else. I always write, "We appreciate your confidence in allowing us to help your friend"—or your sister or mother—whoever it might be. "We'll do everything we can to ensure that we get them what they deserve. We will take care of their case and them."

With all the e-mails and texts on smartphones, people really pay attention to a handwritten note, because it's different. People are so busy during the day, and they are bombarded with electronic messages. You see kids sitting at the same table texting each other. It's crazy. But the bottom line is this: people appreciate the personal touch. I've had people say to me, "I can't believe that you took time to handwrite that thank-you note, Mr. Hardison, because I know you're busy."

I get somebody else to address the envelope but I write the card myself. You're building that relationship, and you go on building the preeminence. You want to be the preeminent law firm in your market. You want to stand out from other lawyers. I don't even like typed letters. I think they're too impersonal. E-mails are too impersonal. A handwritten note makes it personal. It's a lost art.

THE PERSONAL TOUCH DOES MAKE A DIFFERENCE.

I go all over the country to consult with lawyers. I see firms spending six, seven figures on marketing, and their referral rates are probably at 25 percent—or maybe 30 percent, if they're lucky. That means two or three out of ten of the cases they take on have come in via referrals. The other 75 to 80 percent is coming in through marketing and advertising, which they pay for. In our firm, even though we spend seven figures on marketing and advertising, 46 percent of our cases still come from referrals. The personal touch does make a difference. I might write two or three thank-you notes a day, and 40 or 50 a month. It's proven—it's not just me theorizing. I know this works.

And it doesn't take more than two minutes. I have five or six sentences that I use. I change it up every now and then, but the overall message remains the same. If it's for someone I know, I might personalize it a little more by writing, "Say hello to your wife," or "I hope your kids are doing well," or something like that. It could not be easier or more effective. The more cases we can get for less money, the more I can pay my lawyers. I hope that is a motivator for them to send out handwritten notes of their own, too. They all do it. It's just a part of our firm's culture.

The bottom line is, when I send the note, I'm acknowledging the referral. Another thing I like to do is include a thank-you on the front of our newsletter, which goes out every other month. Also, at the bottom of the newsletter, I print a list of everybody who has referred a case to us since the last newsletter went out. I publicly acknowledge them.

(See the sample newsletter below.)

People like to see their name in print. Not only do I send the card, but then I publicly acknowledge the referral, too. They know I appreciate it. That gets them to like me even more, and I'm going to get even more referrals from them. So, it's the little things sometimes. The key is that people are going to refer people to lawyers they know, like, and trust, and I'm just giving you some examples of things you can do to get people to know, like, and trust you.

THE NUMBER-ONE THING I WOULD TELL A LAWYER TO SPEND MONEY ON – A MONTHLY NEWSLETTER.

Most lawyers' egos have them believing that once they've represented you, you're going to remember them forever. But even when you do a great job, people forget. The best way to remedy that is through newsletters and e-zines. When I tell lawyers this, they say, "It's just too much money. It's not direct response. It's wasted money. I can't afford it." But this is the one thing a lawyer should absolutely do. This is the number one thing I would tell a lawyer to spend money on — a monthly newsletter. Not everybody can afford TV or radio. If you spend any money on marketing, start with a monthly newsletter. They work.

Don't make the newsletter all about legal issues. People don't want to read that. There are three keys to an effective newsletter: (1) Write it on a fifth to seventh-grade level, (2) Only make 25 percent of it about law, and, of course, (3) Acknowledge referrals. The purpose of the newsletter is to maintain awareness—not to show how great you are, or whether Senate Bill 236 passed. Instead, include things like tips on how to get stains out of clothes, a crossword puzzle, or a contest with a drawing and prizes. This gets people interested, to the point where they look forward to receiving the newsletter. That fosters top-of-mind awareness. It keeps your name in front of people.

You might have a recipe of the month. You might spotlight an employee or client, if they give you their permission, and describe an unusual case. But again, don't include a lot of "law" in your newsletter.

On the front page of our law firm newsletter, I usually include something personal about myself because I'm creating that relationship with readers. Recently, I wrote about my daughter getting married and the fact that her boyfriend proposed in a helicopter, and I included pictures of it. I wrote, "I have to go to a lot of parties, which I'm really not crazy about, but I'm so happy for my daughter and she picked a great guy." So now they know that Ken's got a daughter who is getting married, and they feel like they know me. I'm sharing personal stuff about myself, but it's all in the best interests of the firm.

If you can't afford to produce a monthly newsletter, do it at least quarterly. I like to do it at least every other month, and I love reinforcing the fact that I'm my clients' trusted legal advisor, that I love referrals, and that I appreciate their business and any future business they can send my way. You can also send out an e-newsletter online, but don't do that alone. Always send out a written newsletter, too. It doesn't have to be long—two or four pages is fine. You just want to get your name out there. It doesn't have to be extra costly. You can produce it in black-and-white. You can do it as fancy as you want to, or as cheap as you want to. The main thing is, you want your name out there and your contact information out there.

Preeminent Resource

Lynn McDowell, founder of Premier Print Marketing, provides an excellent "done for you" newsletter to develop the kind of connection with current and former clients that will lead to an increase in referrals.

Website: www.premierprintmarketing.com, Phone: 877-860-9807

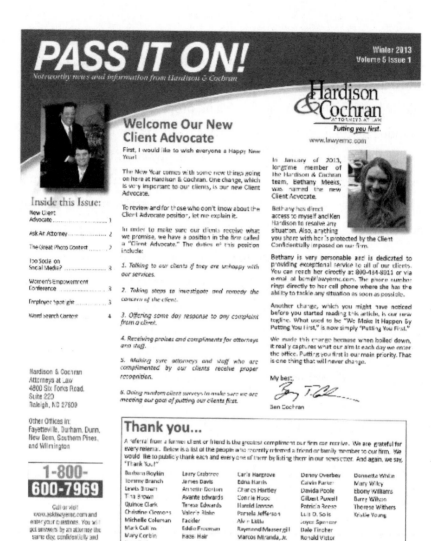

BRANDING

In the overall picture of branding, how do you create a compelling message? Lawyers get this wrong all the time. You see them in the Yellow Pages or on TV and they talk about how great they are. They're in the top 40 under 40, and Super Lawyers and they're AVVO rated, and this and that. But people don't care about that.

Consumers just don't care. What they want to know is, "What's in it for me?" In other words, people don't care about features; they care about benefits. So you've got to create what is called a unique selling proposition. Some people call it "differentiation."

As consumers, we get pounded with thousands of messages a day. It all gets cluttered, so you've got to stand out. I hear lawyers all the time saying, "Well, you know, we all do the same thing. We're interchangeable." Not true! There are so many ways to stand out. Think of a simple concept like a pencil with an eraser on it. A feature on that pencil is the eraser. The benefit of that eraser is the ability to not have to start over from the very beginning of a document every time you make a small error. So the eraser saves you time. That's the benefit.

But then there are more benefits that flow out of that time saved. It means you can make more money in less time, which means you can take more time off, which means you can go on vacations, which means you can go out and have a few drinks and a nice, relaxing dinner. Whatever your thing is, that's the benefit. And that's what is going on in people's minds. So don't just tell people what a great pencil you have, or how great the eraser on that pencil is. Tell them what it can do for them.

USP (UNIQUE SELLING PROPOSITION)

Imitation may be the sincerest form of flattery, but when it comes to marketing your law firm and beating your competition, it falls flat. A large majority of lawyers assume that copying their competitor's ads will help them compete with them. Don't fall into this trap. This is ineffective and costly, and it gives your law firm no competitive advantage in the marketplace.

In 1961, Rosser Reeves wrote a book called *Reality in Advertising* that revolutionized the marketing industry. The book was so influential that it became a college textbook for marketing students. In his book, Reeves announced the idea that every business, product, or service absolutely must have a "USP" or a "Unique Selling Proposition." He maintained that focusing on the USP in every advertising and marketing effort was key to creating an effective and cohesive advertising and marketing campaign.

What is a USP? It's a compelling marketing message that dramatically sets you apart from your competitors and boldly broadcasts the unique benefits that your legal services provide. It's the number-one benefit, or total of all benefits, that differentiates you and your law firm from all other law firms in your market.

Simply put, a USP is:

- An overt, unique claim about your law firm or a promise of benefits of your legal services.
- A statement that impressively positions you as distinctly different from your competitors.
- A statement that is so strong, attractive, and compelling that it motivates prospects to choose your firm over all others.

Basically, a USP answers this basic question—*Why should I do business with your law firm rather than with your competitors, or, better yet, why should I hire a lawyer at all?*

Why do you need a USP? Because your potential prospects are getting hammered every day with hundreds of ads from your competitors! They all say the same things, *"We're tough and aggressive,"*

"We care," "Free consultation," "We don't get paid unless we win." These ads clutter the airwaves and have consumers' brains spinning, because everyone is saying the same thing. No wonder prospective clients don't know who to hire—no one stands out! How can a prospective client choose the law firm that's right for them when they all look the same, sound the same, and make the same promises? The fact that the legal advertising space is cluttered with cookie-cutter ads and the same messages over and over is actually a good thing for you. This gives you a golden opportunity to stand out from your competition. How? You get a USP. Now.

Most lawyers I talk to say, "Ken, we do all the same things our competitors are doing," or, "We are bound by laws and regulations on what we can do and what we can say to potential clients," or, "We don't have much choice, there really is no way to stand out from the crowd."

My answer to those excuses is simply this—"It can be done." Is it easy? Not necessarily, but with the right mindset and tools you can create a USP for your firm that will increase your return on your investment from your advertising three to ten times what it presently yields.

To develop a powerful and effective USP, you must think like a potential client. What keeps them up at night? What is their big problem that you can solve? What is the headache your firm can cure? Above all, focus on answering the potential client's most critical question—*what's in it for me?* The only way to answer that question is to sell the "benefits" of your law firm, and not the "features" of your legal services.

Remember the eraser-on-the-pencil example. The feature of that eraser is that is will erase your mistakes. The benefit is that you save yourself time and effort, because you don't have to rewrite everything from the beginning if you make a mistake. The feature is the eraser, but the benefit is the time you save. See the difference?

How about a benefit versus a feature in action in a USP? Let's use Domino's Pizza as our example. They advertise "piping hot pizza delivered in 30 minutes or less." The benefit is hot, instead of cold, pizza, and fast, instead of slow, delivery. By focusing on the benefits, they are showing the consumers what's in it for them. Every consumer now knows that if you order Domino's, you'll get hot pizza delivered fast. This is how Domino's differentiated itself from the other competitors in the pizza-delivery business and created a multi-million-dollar operation.

Note, Domino's never claimed to be the *best-tasting* pizza. They focused on their target market—people who want and need pizza fast and cheap. Focus on your prospective clients. Your USP should tell them that you're the firm that can give them what they need. Period. This is key. You must know what your prospective clients want in order to create a USP that works.

Why do people resist hiring a lawyer? Many do so because they lack funds and are afraid they will be taken advantage of. I used this fear to create the USP for my own law firm. We use "30-Day Client Service Satisfaction Guarantee—No questions and no fees." We give new clients the opportunity to try our firm for 30 days. If at any time during the first 30 days they aren't 100 percent satisfied with the way we have treated them and their case, then they can ask for their file back with no fees. (See www.CarolinaSSDLawyers.com.)

While it's a compelling offer in and of itself, the benefit to the potential client is that they can "try us" and change lawyers without the fear of having to pay for two lawyers if they aren't 100 percent happy. In our USP, I incorporated the concept of risk reversal. By giving them a 30-day guarantee with no fees, we take all of the risk, leaving the client able and willing to take action risk free. The benefit, again, is that they are not stuck with a law firm that they are not happy with.

SELECT YOUR USP AND STICK WITH IT! USE IT IN YOUR MARKETING AND ADVERTISING. IT SHOULD BECOME YOUR MANTRA.

The key thing to remember when developing and using a USP is this: *You can't be all things to all people.* Select your USP and stick with it! You should use it in everything you do to market and advertise your firm. It should become your mantra—and you should use the heck out of it! It is, after all, who you are.

When lawyers say we all do the same things and are constrained by rules and regulations so our hands are tied, I always disagree. What we do may be the same, but how we do it is a different question altogether. You could have a "Client Bill of Rights" or a Client Advocate. You could even offer to handle property damage for free. All these things could be molded into your USP.

You could be the first lawyer in your market to promote a particular benefit that all other lawyers in your market provide but don't necessarily promote. Sometimes, when everyone is providing the same service, no one bothers to promote it. Why is this? Why would you not promote something that would cause a prospective client to hire you? So what if everyone else does it? If no one is promoting it, you should be the first to shout it from the rooftops! If no one is talking about it, how do potential clients know you're doing it? Let it set you apart. This is called "creating a preemptive USP."

In other words, you are promoting what you do, and providing people with the facts about those services. Even though all of the other lawyers in your market do the same thing, you will have given yourself a competitive advantage simply by stating that you do it. If you say it first, you'll establish a preeminent market position and will be perceived as the market leader. Other firms who try to follow suit and quickly claim the same thing will be considered "copycats" and "me too" firms, and will only end up advertising, in essence, for you.

For example, if your USP is, "We will handle your P.P. or Med Pay Claim for free," even if every other lawyer in town does that, you can be the first one to say it out loud and use it to differentiate yourself and how you handle cases. This is how you execute a pre-emptive USP. (For a more-detailed guide on how to create a USP for your law firm, visit: www.CreateAUSP.com.)

A TAGLINE IS A SLOGAN. A USP IS A PROMISE OF SERVICES.

Remember: A USP is not the same thing as a tagline. People get those two mixed up. A tagline is something like, "Putting you first." That's the tagline we use at our firm. A tagline is a slogan. A USP is a promise of services. You need to tell people about the unique benefits of your firm and you do that with USPs.

Take Schlitz Brewery, for example. Back in the 1960s, Schlitz was about to go bankrupt. One of the premiere advertising agencies, Ogilvy, went in and looked at their plant. They said, "Man, you guys are steam washing these bottles before you put the beer in them. That's pretty neat."

The brewery said, "Everybody does that."

Ogilvy said, "But nobody knows it."

So they made up this big advertising campaign about how their bottles were steam washed. Every other beer manufacturer out there was doing the same thing, but Schlitz was calling attention to it. They made a big deal out of it and they made a huge comeback as a company. And they're still in business today. That's a prime example of a "preemptive USP." You're saying, "Hey, we do this." And then if anybody else says, "Well, we do it too," it makes it sound like they're just copying you. He who is first wins the race, right?

Once, I advised a lawyer to say, "We handle property damage for free."

He said, "All the lawyers in our market do that."

I said, "Does anybody advertise it or make a big deal out of it?"

He said, "No."

I said, "Well, that's what you ought to do. That's your USP."

STANDING OUT FROM THE CLUTTER

For my own firm, I went on TV and offered a 100 percent client-satisfaction guarantee, which scares the hell out of lawyers. Everybody thought I was crazy. But man, it really increased our calls. I said, "No lawyer can ethically guarantee the outcome of your case, and neither can we. But we can guarantee that you will be completely satisfied with the way we treat you and your case, and if you're not completely satisfied during the first 30 days that you hire us, you can come and get your file. No cost. No fees. That's our 100 percent client-satisfaction guarantee from us to you."

But here's the deal. Any client can come get their file any time they want to. A contract with a lawyer is the only contract in the United States that is not enforceable, because of ethics. But no clients know that. So they think that within 30 days after they begin, they might have some costs and they might owe some fees. What I did was something I call risk reversal. I reversed the risk, but I also made a statement. No other lawyer is doing this. We stand out. So I'm accomplishing three things with that ad.

Number one, I'm standing out from all of the clutter and I'm making a guarantee, which is risk reversal. Some people, when they're choosing a lawyer, might like you but not know yet if they can trust you. This gives them a little grace period. "Try us out for thirty days." If you don't like us, you don't have to give us anything. Just take your file back. You don't pay us anything up front because we're on contingency.

Lawyers thought I was crazy to advertise that. The reason most lawyers don't want to do it is they are not trying to build a pre-eminent law firm. What we do in our firm, and any firm that I've ever run, is that we talk to the client. We paper them to death. We keep them in the loop about what's going on. We fast-track the case. We get the ball rolling. We jump-start it. We've got systems and an infrastructure set up to do just that. They're seeing all this stuff in the first 30 days and they're thinking, "These guys are great." So I also achieved their trust. That's number two.

And then the third thing I've accomplished is that I've given great client service. My staff knows that we've got to do that, and in offering that guarantee for 10 years now, we've had maybe two people take their files back. Think about how many people hired us, people who had been sitting on a fence until they heard about our guarantee. Lawyers look nice. They look approachable. But people often wonder not only about which lawyer to hire, but if they need to even hire a lawyer at all. The insurance companies tell them that they don't need a lawyer, that the lawyer will take all of the money.

This is where a USP comes in. It tells people what the main benefit to them is going to be, and it helps you differentiate yourself from other lawyers. Beyond that, it convinces people that they actually do need a lawyer in the first place. I hear a lot of lawyers saying, "We're tough, we're aggressive, we care." People hear that from everybody and they become deaf to it. So you've got to get creative and get your message out.

FOLLOW-UP

Follow-up is really important. It is essential, but lawyers are terrible at it. Why? They're busy. They forget. They're spending their time trying to get a new hot lead. Some lawyers think that following up is unprofessional, and some of them think they're too good for it. Their egos tell them that people are just going to call them back. Some lawyers don't want to be pushy. Or they feel like they're selling themselves and they don't want to do that. But I think the biggest reason lawyers don't follow up is that they just don't realize how important it is.

Studies have shown that it takes six to seven touches for somebody to really recognize who you are, and get your message. If they see you just one time and call you, and they haven't made up their mind about how you were on that first call, chances are, unless you do some follow-up, they're not going to call you back. It's not unethical to follow up once somebody has already contacted you. A lot of lawyers think it's unethical, but once again, this is where they are wrong. Once a person contacts you, they've officially come to you for advice. Now you have an ethical obligation — and a moral obligation — to help that person if you think you can. If you truly think you can help that person, then you owe it to yourself and to them to give them an opportunity to hire you. And if they don't want to hire you, you should at least direct them to somebody else who is competent and can help them.

People need help. If I talk to a plumber about plumbing my house, and I say, "I think I'll just do it myself," that guy has a moral obligation to help me because he knows I'm going to screw it up. I'm going to cost myself ten times as much as I would have paid him to do it right in the first place. Some businesses are great at communicating this. But most businesses are terrible at it. Lawyers are the worst.

What most lawyers don't understand is, you don't have to be salesy. When I say you should follow up, I don't mean that you should harass people to death. All you have to do is keep educating people, and sending them e-mails and reports, and letting them know what their options are, what the possibilities are. So how do you do this? You've got to have a system, as I mentioned earlier. You've got to systematize everything. There are hundreds of software products that systematize. Aweber. Infusionsoft. SalesForce.

I like Infusionsoft, but that's just my preference. Some people think it's too complicated, and it might be. Some people use iContact. But I think you ought to have at least eight follow-ups during the first 12 days because, as I mentioned, it takes six or seven touches to get someone to make a decision if they're undecided when they call you that first time. And then I like to follow up with another seven to ten touches over the next 60 days, and then add them to my e-zine or newsletter lists.

Even if they don't hire me this time — they might try to do it themselves or get somebody else and have a terrible experience — I will be on their radar for next time. If they have a bad experience with someone else, or if they do it themselves and fail, they might think, "Damn, I wish I would have hired Hardison. He had this wealth of knowledge and I didn't. I listened to my cousin Susie and I hired Joe Blow down the street. He was terrible. So the next time I need a lawyer, or my child gets into an accident, I'm going to hire Hardison, because they know what they're doing at his firm. They send me all kinds of information. I keep seeing their name. They're doing good stuff in the community. They're talking to groups everywhere, about everything." Do you see how this can help?

A "touch" could be a phone call, a letter, or an e-zine. It could be anything that communicates with a prospective client. They've got to raise their hand first and say, "I'm interested," or else your contact with them would be an unethical solicitation. But once they've gotten in touch with you, you're home free. The more you can mix it up, the better off you are. People respond to different communications differently. I always like to follow up in the same manner that a person contacted us. If we get a lead off of the Internet, then e-mail is probably the best way to follow up on that lead and contact that person. That's probably how they prefer to communicate. If they call us, then we should call them back when we follow up.

Sometimes you can send an e-mail and say, "Do you want us to send you this free book?" Or you can send them a letter asking the same question. If they call you to say "yes," then you can call them back to ask if they received that book. Make sure they received it two or three days after you mailed it, and then ask them if they have any questions, or if they have read it. "If you have any questions, we have one of our lawyers available for you any time." That's not hard selling. That's just using education-based marketing.

You're doing follow-ups, but you're not explicitly selling. You're educating; you're creating trust. You're not being pushy. When you think of all of the things that lawyers worry about doing, if you can do this the right way — what I call the professional, ethical way — then there's nothing to worry about. A lot of lawyers don't do it this way, and some of them are unethical. They've got runners who go to hospitals and wait outside. Those are the lawyers who give all of us a bad name, and that's not the way it should be done. You don't want runners.

CHAPTER FIVE

During Representation

Most lawyers think about building preeminence as it relates to "before representation," but probably only a small percentage of them think about it as something they can work on "during representation." Jay Abraham coined the phrase "the strategy of preeminence." He's a mentor of mine, and I think he's a brilliant marketing mind and businessman. He teaches the strategy of preeminence, and says that to attain it, you have to change the way you think about being a lawyer and practicing law. You must quit thinking that you're just a purveyor of legal services, and start thinking about what you ultimately want to become — a trusted legal advisor. You want to be seen by all people, especially your clients and past clients, as their problem solver. As their helper. As their trusted legal advisor.

You want them to know that if they ever have a legal problem, they just have to pick up the phone and call you. Some lawyers disagree with me on this. They say, "I don't have time for that. I don't want to deal with all of these little questions and concerns." These lawyers are short-sighted. Think about all of the referral fees that those lawyers are missing. I might not do malpractice. I might not do mass torts. I might not do asbestos cases, but if I practice the strategy of preeminence, in which I am someone's trusted legal advisor and they call me any time they have a legal problem, think of all the good that will come from that, even if I'm not getting referral fees. I can refer domestic cases and criminal cases, and I've already set up all of those referral networks. These lawyers are going to reciprocate and send me cases. You have to see the big picture. That's why it's so important.

EVERYTHING YOU DO SHOULD BE FOR THAT CLIENT'S BENEFIT.

Everything you do should be for that client's benefit, their advantage, their improvement, their enhancement, their enrichment, their betterment, and their well-being. You want to be considered their counselor, their advisor, and their fiduciary. When you refer them to someone, refer them to the best lawyer you know for that kind of work. The reciprocation will take care of itself. It's sort of on auto-pilot. Just make sure that you take care of the client first and foremost. Always keep their best interests in mind. I always put this phrase in my newsletter, "We want you to think of us as your legal advisor, and if you have any legal problems, even if we don't handle it, we'll get you to somebody who's competent and can handle it." I always tell people that same thing when I meet with them. I tell all my lawyers to tell people, too. This is how to build a preeminent law firm!

BE THE GO-TO PERSON

People want to talk to people they know, like, and trust. They would rather pick up the phone and call me than anyone else. Say they get a speeding ticket. Well, I don't handle speeding tickets, but I can get them to somebody who does. They know that, and that's why they call me first. It's like that client I was representing on a criminal matter who all of a sudden had a broken arm. If I had created the strategy of preeminence back when I was first representing him, he would have called me anyway. He didn't, because I was young, and I didn't know what I was doing. Now, when somebody has something they need help with, no matter what it is, I want them to know that they can call me. And if I can't handle it, I can get them to somebody who can, and hopefully I will get a referral fee out of it. Think of all of the millions of dollars I have made by doing that one small thing.

Every paralegal, staffer, and even the mailroom clerk in our office has a list of legal services. When somebody calls and they need a lawyer, if we don't do the kind of work they need, we consult the list. In each city, we have two or three lawyers we know who handle certain types of law, and we refer cases to them. We give those callers three names. They might ask, "Who do you like the best?" We'll tell them. We've got them ranked one, two, and three. You have to train your clients. You've also got to live it. You can't just talk it. You've got to actually do it. You've got to look at this as a relationship. This is not a one-night stand. You want to create a permanent relationship. You want to be the go-to legal advisor for these people and their families for the rest of your life.

CREATING CLIENT LOYALTY IS A LONG ROMANCE, NOT A ONE-NIGHT STAND.

When I was growing up, my father had one lawyer. If he had a problem he went to him. He could handle it. But then, everybody got specialized, and marketing started getting more popular, and TV rose in prominence, followed by social media. Now the TV has 500 channels and we get thousands of messages every day. Everything is fragmented and specialized. Everybody is an expert on one thing: specialist, specialist, specialist. It happened in the medical field first. It has now happened with law. What you want to try to do is rise above that and become a trusted legal advisor.

If you do it at the beginning, when you sign up a client, you can start to sprinkle your message into your letters and newsletters, and plant the seed. You have to train your staff but you also have to train your clients. This is what you should want, and you have to instill it in your law firm's culture. You can't say, "I don't have time. We don't do this. Bye." You have to say, "How can I help you? We don't do that but I can put you in touch with a great lawyer who does." This will set you apart from your competition. Set this up as a part of your core values, and reiterate it to your staff members and your lawyers.

They must know how important this is. If you don't make it important to yourself, it's not going to be important to them. I can tell you that right now. Instead of just having satisfied clients, I want to create loyal clients, for two reasons: I want to be their legal advisor for life, and I want them to refer me everybody they possibly can. That is how the tree grows and the branches spread out.

CHAPTER SIX

Creating Client Loyalty

P otential clients are bombarded by thousands of messages a day meant to persuade their spending habits. Whether it's the billboard they drive past every day, the label on the bottle of Pepsi they're drinking, or the Cadillac emblem on the car they're stuck behind in traffic, these visual messages are meant to create top-of-mind awareness and persuade the consumer to buy a certain product or service. With such as onslaught of messages, it's no wonder that consumer habits can change at the drop of a hat.

CLIENT LOYALTY IS OF THE UTMOST IMPORTANCE.

CLIENT LOYALTY

Simplistic messages that create top-of-mind awareness cannot sway the loyal client. While the competition is spending mega-dollars to increase client volume, many of them are forgetting the importance of their existing clients. Forgetting this will almost certainly lead to a number of unsatisfied clients, who will likely never become loyal clients.

A loyal client and a satisfied client are not to be confused. While client satisfaction is an element of loyalty, a client could be satisfied and still feel no connection to you or your firm. A loyal client experiences five things:

1. The overall satisfaction of doing business with your law firm
2. The willingness to build a relationship with you and your law firm
3. The willingness to be a repeat client
4. The willingness to recommend you to others
5. The reluctance to switch to another law firm

In order for your clients to achieve those five things, there are 10 rules that you and your employees should follow every day:

1. GREET CLIENTS PROMPTLY

A survey timed the number of seconds people waited to be greeted in several businesses. Researchers then asked clients how long they had been waiting. In every case, the client's estimate of the time elapsed was much longer than the actual time. A client waiting 30 or 40 seconds often felt like it had been three or four minutes. Time drags when people are waiting. Thus, one of the things we can do to greet clients properly is not put them on hold. When they call or make their appointment answer the phone on its first ring when being paged by the receptionist, and be on time for your appointments.

This is a good time to tell you that one of your best investments is a good receptionist. This person can make or break your firm, depending on how well she deals with people. Give your reception-ist great latitude to get the calls answered, and if the rest of the firm doesn't fall in line, afford this person an open-door policy. I have found time and time again that the receptionist knows if you are meeting client satisfaction goals.

2. APPLY GOOD CONVERSATION SKILLS

It is always nice to talk to people like they are in your living room. In general, people are intimidated by lawyers in law offices. It should be your job to make them feel comfortable, since they have already been through a traumatic event. Something to break the ice would be the weather; for example, "Isn't the sunshine just beautiful?" or, "The snowfall's great, isn't it?" Look for clues about the client's interest. Also, you must understand that interaction means that both parties have an opportunity to participate. If one party monopolizes the conversation, both sides lose.

Some preferred topics are what we refer to as small talk. Americans prefer to talk about weather, sports, jobs, mutual acquaintances, and past experiences, especially ones they have in common with their conversation partners. Most Americans are taught to avoid discuss-ing politics or religion, especially with people they do not know well. Sex, bodily functions, and emotional problems, considered very personal topics, are likely to be discussed only with close friends or professionals trained to help.

3. BUILD A RAPPORT WITH THE CLIENT

Remember that you are building a relationship with your client. He must know that his case is the top priority, and that you are there for him.

- Be a good listener.
- Relate to what he is going through.
- Invite feedback.

4. BE SINCERE AND SHOW EMPATHY TO THE OTHER PERSON

I have preached for years, *There, but for the grace of God, go I.* You should understand that these people are hurting and coming to you for assistance.

5. USE GOOD PHONE TECHNIQUES

A key to successful phone use is simply to remember that your client cannot see you. Your challenge is to use your voice to make up for all of the lost nonverbal communication. The best ways to use the phone effectively are:

- Give the caller your name. Let the caller know who you are, just as you would in a face-to-face situation.
- Smile into the phone. Somehow people can hear us smile over the phone! Some telephone pros place a mirror in front of them while they are on the phone.
- Keep your caller informed. If you need to look up information, tell the client what you are doing. Don't leave them holding a dead phone with no clue as to whether you are still with them.

- Invite the caller to get to the point. Use questions such as, "How can I assist you today?" or, "What can I do for you?"
- Commit to the requests of the caller; tell the caller specifically what you will do and when you will get back to them.
- Thank the caller. This lets the caller know when the conservation is over.
- Let your voice fluctuate in tone, rate, and volume. You hold people's attention by putting a little life into your voice. Express honest reactions in expressive ways. Let your voice tone be natural and friendly.
- Use *hold* carefully. People hate being put on hold. It is always necessary to explain why you are asking someone to hold, and you should break in periodically to let them know that they haven't been forgotten. If what you are doing will take longer than a few minutes, ask the caller if you can call them back. Write down your commitment to call them back, and make sure to do it.
- Use friendly, common, tactful words. Never accuse the client of anything, and never convey that his request is an imposition.

6. ENJOY PEOPLE AND THEIR DIVERSITY

Every person is different; each has a unique personality. People who tend to bug us the most are the ones who are not like us. Recognize this, accept this diversity and learn to enjoy it. Know that people's needs are basically the same; similarly, when we treat them like guests, with dignity and courtesy, it creates goodwill most of the time.

7. CALL PEOPLE BY THEIR NAMES

People love to hear their names. Think about the times when someone unexpectedly addressed you by your name... didn't it feel good? Didn't you feel less like a number and more like someone who is valued? People appreciate it when you make the effort to learn their name and use it. Here are some ways to make the most of name-calling:

- When appropriate, introduce yourself to the client and ask his or her name.
- Avoid being overly familiar too quickly. It's normally safe to address people as Mr. Smith or Mrs. Jones. It could be seen as rude if you call them by their first name too quickly.
- If you aren't sure how to pronounce the name, ask the client.
- If a person has an unusual or interesting name, comment on it in a positive way.
- If a person shares a name with someone in your family or with a friend, comment on that.

People are usually proud of their names and will feel honored when you acknowledge them. Take time to learn and use your clients' names.

8. WEAR YOUR SMILE WHEN A CLIENT COMES INTO THE OFFICE

Always put on your smile when somebody comes into the office. Be complimentary. Complimenting takes only a second, and can add enormous goodwill. If you don't do this often, get into the habit of saying something complimentary to each of your clients. Safe grounds for sincere compliments are as follows:

- Some article of clothing they are wearing
- Their children
- Their behavior
- Something they own
- Their helpfulness. For example, "Thank you for filling out the forms so carefully, that will help."

9. FISH FOR NEGATIVE FEEDBACK

What? Fish for negative feedback? Exactly. Negative feedback is the kind that helps you improve. In client service, there is no neutral gear; we either move forward or we slip backward. The best way to get feedback is to let clients know that you really want their honest opinion... good or bad news... and provide ways for them to tell you.

A good way to do this is to use open-ended questions when people express their ideas. An open-ended question cannot be answered with a simple yes, no, or a one-worded response. Below are common questions you hear every day in businesses that can be easily changed to open-ended:

Instead of saying:	Say:
"How was everything?"	"What else can I do for you?"
"Can I get you something else?"	"What else can I get for you?"
"Will that be all?"	"What else can I do for you?"
"Was everything satisfactory?"	"What else could we do better to serve you?"
"Did we meet your needs?"	"How else can we be of help?"

10. LIVE BY THE GOLDEN RULE

I have preached this ever since I started practicing law. Simply put: treat people the way you would want to be treated.

These rules are so simple, yet it constantly amazes me that other law firms do not put them into play. I have come to realize that it's the leadership's responsibility to set the standards. These rules, as the basis of a client loyalty program, must be non-negotiable. You absolutely, 100 percent, must be willing to terminate your highest income producer or your best non-lawyer, if they don't believe in client loyalty. I have done it, and I have never regretted it.

CHAPTER SEVEN

Tactics to Give an Unbelievable Client Experience

There's an old saying, "Under Promise, Over Deliver" and that is a good thought to carry with you in all of your business practices.

Before we had laws, rules, and courts, we had promises—the assurance that something will be done.

These are four reasons we make promises:

1. To create obligation
2. To regulate and direct behavior
3. To reduce uncertainty
4. To build trust

As I mentioned earlier, people hire and refer to lawyers they like, know, and trust. If you think about it, trust is the big issue when people are hiring lawyers. As lawyers, we want to build a relationship of trust with prospects and with our clients. Even if you don't win their case, if a client trusts you, they will return or refer you a future case. If you really think about it, we are not selling legal services, but trust. Promises signal to the outside world your level of trustworthiness. This is why under-promising and over-delivering is so important. In all the stages of representation, "trust" is the key to building preeminence! That's why I titled this book *Under Promise, Over Deliver: How to Build a Preeminent Law Firm in Your Market.* It's all about building trust, which creates the relationships that in turn build you into the preeminent law firm in your market!

Big promises create big expectations. When you don't fulfill those promises, you lose the trust of the people you made the promises to. On the other hand, if you exceed those expectations, you strengthen the trust. Everyone benefits.

Never try to tell people just what they want to hear. Here's the way I look at it. If you under promise, and for some reason things don't work out as you thought, then people are not going to be disappointed. But if you happen to do your regular standard performance, then you've exceeded their expectations. The idea is not to set the expectations too high. Most times, you can exceed them. Under Promise, Over Deliver. I really believe in that. A lot of lawyers over-promise to begin with, and that's where they falter. They're terrible with their client service. They tell clients whatever they want to hear just to get them to sign on the dotted line, and that's a huge mistake. You're setting yourself up for failure down the road.

UNDER PROMISE, OVER DELIVER.

I'm going to share with you some tactics that will help you give unbelievable client experiences. These are things I've done over the years and they have worked.

ADVOCATE HOTLINE

I actually created a client advocate hotline. We tell people to call us if they have any problems dealing with a lawyer, a staff member, or anybody at the firm. If they think they're getting the runaround or they're just not happy about something, they can call this hotline 24/7, and it will go right to my office manager's cell phone. She's had years and years of experience, and she will investigate the complaint.

Half of the time, the complaints are unfounded. Sometimes they're valid, but the thing is, you've got the number out there at all times. Instead of just talking about giving great client service, you're actually doing it. And that's one of the ways you can do it. Another thing we did was create a Client Bill of Rights, and you can see that at www.CarolinaSSDLawyers.com.

CELEBRATE A CLIENT

We always require 30 or 45-day client update calls. For the lawyer, it's usually 45 days, and for the staff it's usually 30 days. In addition, my former partner Ben Cochran came up with a great idea called the "Celebrate a Client" contest for staff. Instead of trying to get people off the phone after we have secured their business, our staff members ask them about what's going on with their family, and what else is happening in their lives. Most times, it's bad stuff. But maybe their kid earned a spot on a ball team, or maybe they got an award. Maybe their daughter is getting married. Our staff people fill out a form and turn them into the office manager, and then our lawyers actually write a little note to the client, congratulating them on whatever great thing happened.

The staff person who gets the most of these every month gets a $200 bonus. So you're incentivizing them to do things, but really it's creating this great relationship in which the client actually becomes more than just a client. It shows the client that this is going to be a permanent relationship, and it's about more than just the case. It says, "We care about you as a person. You're family." To me, that's just golden. The only thing I'm upset about is that I didn't think of it myself. It's one of the best ideas I've ever heard concerning relationship building. It's also a great marketing tool. It does so many things. It's probably my favorite tactic of all. On top of it all, we have monthly meetings and talk about it, and bring in lunch. It provides nothing but positive feelings for everyone involved.

CLIENT ADVISORY PANEL

Another tactic that has worked really well is our Client Advisory Panel. We go to different cities and sponsor a dinner for our best referrers. All lawyers have to be there and we actually go around the table and talk to the people who have referred clients to us in the past. We have dinner and we give them a little survey. We ask them what they are hearing about us on the streets, and we listen to their feedback. We ask if anybody has any complaints, or if they have heard of anybody who has complaints about us. We ask if there is anything they think we could do to make the firm a better place for our clients. These people, in effect, become our honorary board of directors for client services. This creates great loyalty. It recognizes these people. It makes them part of our firm, and it's going to make them want to refer us more clients. That was my idea, and I think it's a great one. Maybe it's not as good as the "Celebrate a Client" idea, but it's still a good one. Maybe you'll come up with an even better idea.

Finally, you can always do surveys. A lot of people do them just once or twice. I like to do them after 30, 90, and 180 days. Usually 30 days after a case is complete is when you can tell the most, because people don't want to upset the applecart before that. They want to be quiet until everything is done, and then they will tell you what they really think. Just be systematic with whatever time frame you choose.

CHAPTER EIGHT

After Representation

We've talked about what to do "before representation" and "during representation," and now here's what probably 98 percent of lawyers miss the boat on: "after representation." They get the client in. They have a sit-down with them at the firm. They get them to hire them. They work really hard to give them high-quality, excellent legal service and client service. The client gets a check, and the lawyers close the file and forget about that person forever. And then the lawyers go back to square one, which is starting all over again trying to find new, qualified leads.

REFERRALS ARE GOLD IN YOUR POCKET

These lawyers are missing out. It's tragic, because who better to get referrals and repeat business from than former clients? They have friends, they have families, and they know people. They say everybody has a circle of at least 50 people, and some influential people have a circle of 250 people. You want to nurture lifetime relationships. A lot of marketing gurus talk about the lifetime value of a client. If you know your average fee on a worker's comp case is $10,000, then you should not think that the value of that client is $10,000.00. That's shortsighted.

I look at the lifetime value of a client as follows: If I do a great job and exceed their expectations, then they're probably going to refer two or three people to me over their lifetime. That would make the lifetime value of that client $30,000 or $40,000 instead of just $10,000. So if you focus on marketing to these people and developing this relationship after representation, it should translate to at least three times the value of what it took to get that lead originally.

Instead of getting a 10-to-1 return on my investment, I just got a 30-to-1 ROI. Most lawyers are not thinking about cases that way. They're thinking short term. They're losing a lot of money by going back to find new leads, when they could just keep nurturing old clients. You want to orchestrate these referrals by becoming their trusted legal advisor. Once you set it in motion, it takes care of itself.

When somebody refers somebody to you, three things must happen. First, they have to notice that there's a conversation occurring about hiring a lawyer. Next, they have to be thinking about you. And finally, they have to introduce you into the conversation. It's almost like a subtle brainwashing. You want people to know that you like referrals, that you want referrals, and that the biggest compliment anybody could ever pay your law firm would be to refer you a case.

The best way I know how to do that is—ask for it! Once we settle a case and do the settlement disbursement with the client, we take advantage of this ideal time to ask for future referrals. They're very happy 90 percent of the time. They say, "I really appreciate it. What can I do for you?" I say, "You can tell all your friends and family about us, because a referral is the biggest compliment we could receive." As I mentioned earlier, I always make it very clear on the cover of our newsletter how much we love referrals. It's all about indoctrination from the beginning of your representation. You need to tell people what you want. Start sending that message out at the beginning and when you close the file, after they get the results they wanted, you send them a letter.

You do some cross-selling and you let them know, "Hey, we were happy to represent you and we appreciate you giving us the opportunity. We hope that we exceeded your expectations. And, by the way, we handled your worker's comp case but we also do personal injury and we do social security. We welcome referrals. And again, referrals are the biggest compliments you could ever give us and we appreciate them." Then, when they send you a referral, you write the handwritten thank-you note. You thank them in a very intimate and personal way, and the cycle continues.

It's not just one thing. It's everything combined. The more things you can do like that, the more you're going to get them to notice. And if they consider you their trusted legal advisor and you act the part, then they're going to try to help you, because people like to reciprocate.

RECIPROCITY

Let's talk about the reciprocity theory. A number of people are narcissistic and care only about themselves. That's life. But most people want to return favors and do nice things for others. You can't usually tell by looking at someone, so you should treat everyone the same. You have the conversations and put out the message over and over. It pays off. It works.

Next, they have to think about you, and know how to reach you. A case in point: I moved down to Myrtle Beach about five years ago and I was having some plumbing issues. I'm not a plumber, so I went online, did some research, and called a couple of plumbers until I got one to come out right away. It was a minor emergency so I needed someone to fix it immediately.

The guy did a wonderful job. He gave me great service, did everything he needed to fix my problem, was honest, and charged a fair price. I paid him on the spot and thanked him. He gave me his business card. Six months later, I had another plumbing issue, but I had lost that card and for the life of me could not remember who he was. So, back I went to the Internet. But this time, I called a different plumber. I would have loved to call that first plumber, but I just didn't know how to find him.

This new plumber came out, and for the second time in a year I was very lucky. He did a great job, gave me great service, and charged me a fair price. But before he left he did something that the first plumber didn't do. He gave me a magnet with his name and phone number on it. He had fixed my hot water heater, so as he handed me the magnet, he said, "Put this on the hot water heater." Then he gave me a second magnet. He said, "Here's one for your refrigerator. If you need anything, just give me a call day or night and I'll come out here." A few years later I had another problem. Guess whom I called? That's right—the guy on the magnet. Sound familiar? Sound like a concept we've explored in this book?

STAY IN TOUCH

You can also send out greeting cards for birthdays, anniversaries, Valentine's Day, Christmas, Thanksgiving, and Fourth of July. All of these things help you stay in front of people, and none of it seems like selling or soliciting. You're just keeping your name in front of potential referrers. Below is a recent Valentine's card we sent out to our past and present clients.

I love to send Thanksgiving cards, because they arrive before other lawyers' Christmas cards and don't get lost in the clutter. I also like to include a refrigerator magnet with the next year's calendar on it, along with a picture of myself and my law firm's toll-free number and tagline. When people go to their refrigerator, they're going to see that magnet. They might become blind to it, but when it's time to call or recommend a lawyer, they'll remember it. You have to first get them to think about you, right? Then they have to initiate the conversation, and this is where it gets a little bit tricky. You need a tool to do the heavy lifting for you.

I like to use our consumer books. When somebody gets through with a case, I give them several books. If they refer cases to me, I give them even more books. I say, "If you come across somebody who needs me, give them this book. Tell them, 'This is the lawyer I had on my case.'" Just give them some ideas on how to start the conversation. The person's next question is going to be, "Is he any good?" or, "Did he do a good job for you?" If the person is recommending you, those answers are always going to be positive.

My consumer books are written in such a way that they do the sales job for me, so the person handing over the book doesn't need to do any selling. All they've got to do is say, "Hey, this is a great lawyer," or even just, "Hey, this is the lawyer who helped me." The person receiving the book goes, "Okay, this lawyer wrote a book." That instantly makes me an authority figure. It's a great thing for the person doing the introduction, and it's a great thing for me.

Keychains also work. Put your name and phone number on a keychain. Or send people cellphone holders that they can put on the dashboard of their car to keep their phones from slipping. Put your name and number on them and don't be surprised if you get some referrals as a result. A client of yours could be in their car when they get a call from someone with a problem, and they might go, "Hey, I'll call my lawyer. The number is actually right here—I'm looking at it." Making it easy for people to think of you and get hold of you is all part of the big picture.

I can't remember my plumber's phone number, but if somebody wanted a plumber, I'd say "Hey, I haven't got his number right now but I will get it for you when I get home." I would follow up on that, but by that time maybe my friend would have found a different plumber. If that plumber had done the things we do—put his name and number on useful items in my car and at the office—it would be a lot easier for me to give him a referral. If he had given me a book about plumbing, I could have passed it along to someone and said, "Here's a book that my plumber wrote about the eight questions you should ask any plumber before hiring him," or "The secrets that plumbers don't want you to know." A book like that would be a great idea for a plumber, and would make him that much easier to recommend to people. Promotional items such as key chains, calendar magnets, and pill boxes are excellent ways to make it easy for people to call you. We have been using Rusty Dickens for years for these type of promotional products. He gives excellent customer service and is always very competitive with other vendors when it comes to pricing.

Preeminent Resource

Rusty Dickens with Jim Dickens Printing & Promotional Products, Inc. is my choice for any promotional items you may want to promote your firm. From pizza cutters to T-shirts. They are always prompt, courteous, and competively priced.

Website: http://jimdickens.espwebsite.com/

Phone: 252-985-1000

These ideas work for any business or practitioner—financial advisor, doctor, lawyer, loan-service company—it doesn't matter. You can always use these strategies and techniques to stay top-of-mind and establish yourself as the authority in your field.

TESTIMONIALS

Testimonials are also great. Some states will not let you use them in advertisements, but will let you use them with individuals after they've contacted you. Other states let you use them at will. In states where you need to wait for people to contact you first, you can mail or e-mail testimonials to them. Getting great reviews on Yelp and Google is really important, too. The opinion of others is priceless.

WHAT YOU SAY ABOUT YOURSELF IS GOOD, BUT WHAT OTHERS SAY ABOUT YOU IS GOLD.

Of course, we have a system set up for that, because we have a system set up for just about everything. When somebody's case is complete, we try to get them to like us on Facebook and write a Google review or Yelp review, because these things serve as social proof. Remember, "What you say about yourself is good, but what others say about you is gold." I think testimonials can explain better than you can how your firm handles cases and treats clients. Testimonials say, "Not only do I think this firm is great, but look at all of these other people saying it, too."

AC Nielson tells us that something like 85 percent of us make our buying decisions based on word-of-mouth, and this is even more important in our world of non-stop social media. Testimonials and online reviews are very important. Then again, if you do a bad job, word-of-mouth can kill your reputation. There are people out there now actually operating businesses that manage people's reputations. Complete businesses are based on this concept. When someone gets bad reviews, they can hire a company to get the reviews either removed or pushed down so far that people don't see them. The service is expensive and nowhere near as sensible as having a strategy for building a stack of positive reviews. When you have a stack of positive online reviews, they make you look good. You can never have enough of them. Even if you've got 200 of them, that's not too many.

Preeminent Resource

Simon Aronowitz, founder and CEO of "The Testimonial Guru," provides a "done for you" system of obtaining and leveraging testimonials to dramatically increase your law firm's conversions of leads.

Website: www.TestimonialSystems.com

Phone: 843-282-7871

Here is a tip about testimonials. It might seem like a small thing, but it actually has a lot of impact. Instead of attributing a testimonial to just initials, such as "J. H.," give the person's full name. Initials, even when they are a person's real initials, seem made up. People don't always believe the testimonial when they see it attributed to just initials. It's better to put a full name beneath the testimonial, and it's better yet to include a name and town. Even better is name, town, and a picture of the person. Each additional piece of information increases the proof that the person exists and actually said good things about you. It makes it much easier for potential clients to look and say, "That could be me."

I used to get letters from clients who would tell me how thankful they were for the work I had done for them. They would bestow all of these great praises on my law firm. I would scan those letters into our system and put a blurb from them, along with the authors' hometowns and pictures of them, on our website. I also had an icon that people could click on to pull up the actual letters and look at them. It was just more proof that these were real testimonials.

I had no problem asking people for testimonials, and neither should you. I have people call me up and tell me what a great job Suzie or John did on their case. I say, "Do you mind writing me a short note? I can put it in their file, and if you don't mind, and I have your permission, I'd like to use it in our marketing materials." Most people have no problem doing that for you. Many people are even happy to do it.

Testimonials have numerous benefits. I put them in our newsletter, and it makes the people who wrote them feel good. I put them on our website, and they help us attract new business. I put them in the brag-book in the lobby of my office, and they might persuade someone to hire us if they haven't yet made up their mind. Need I say more? So again, it's not just one thing. And these suggestions are not exhaustive by any means. You are limited only by your imagination.

USING NEGATIVE FEEDBACK

Testimonials and praise are great, but don't be afraid of negative feedback. Some lawyers don't want to hear bad news, but I do. I want to hear it, because I can't do a damn thing about it if I don't. Most people who are unhappy with your firm never say a thing to you. They say it to everybody else. I want to know. I want to hear the negative feedback myself. If I don't, I'm never going to build and sustain a preeminent law firm, because I can't get better if I don't know where my weaknesses are. You have to hear the negative feedback, because, let's face it, nobody's perfect. You're going to have people who have bad days. What you want to do is make the necessary changes to improve your firm's reputation.

You can take lemons and make lemonade if you handle everything correctly. You can take a bad situation and turn it into a great one. I had a situation, years ago, in which one of my lawyers dropped the ball. He simply didn't do what he was supposed to do. So naturally, the client called to complain. I turned that situation around and made the client feel good because he knew I really cared. I admonished the lawyer and made him call the client and apologize. Everybody treated that client like he was the King of Siam for the rest of that case. He became one of our raving fans. He has sent us probably a dozen cases since then. If I hadn't known about that first complaint, I couldn't have fixed it. I turned a complaint into 12 referrals over 10 years. This is why I want to hear the negative reviews. I want to know about the problems so I can correct them.

CLIENT APPRECIATION DAY

Client Appreciation Day is one of my favorite ways to make clients feel good. We have a day once a year where we rent a park, hire a band, clowns, and face painters, bring in little rides for kids, fire up the grills, and do a big barbecue. We have raffles and give away prizes. In addition to these door prizes, everyone goes home with a gift: a little portable cooler, a pizza cutter, or an ice-cream scoop. We give away T-shirts with our name on them so our T-shirts can be our walking billboards. We'll have 500 to 1,000 people show up, depending on the weather. We tell people to bring friends — somebody who hasn't used our services — and we mingle with everybody there. They get to meet us and we get to meet them. Clients really appreciate it and we get to meet new people — people who someday might become our clients, and someday after that might refer cases to us. But underneath it all, it's just a nice day appreciated by our clients. It's just us doing something nice for them, and thanking them for being our loyal clients — for letting us be their trusted legal advisor.

CHAPTER NINE

Pitfalls to Watch for Once You Find Success

Say you do all of the things I've talked about and now you're number one, or you're number two, and you're climbing. You're Avis and you're trying harder; you want to be Hertz. You've got to watch out for pitfalls. I've seen it happen to some really good lawyers, and I'm going to list the pitfalls here in no importance of order. These are the things you've got to watch for once you find success.

COMPLACENCY

Resting on your laurels, being satisfied. You can never be satisfied with where you are, because, "If you're not growing, you're dying." You can tone it down and grow gradually, but you can't become complacent. You've got to be willing to try new things, and change. Ten years ago, the Yellow Pages were great. Now, nobody's in the Yellow

Pages. All of the smart lawyers are out of the Yellow Pages and are doing Internet, pay-per-click, and social media. The Internet is still a big deal, but now you've got to be mobile-ready. Fifty-three percent of people who do an Internet search do it on their mobile phones. TV is becoming a lot less effective than it was, so you've got to look at new ways to market your practice.

IF IT AIN'T BROKE, BREAK IT!

You can be making a million dollars a year or five million dollars a year, and you can say, "I'm happy with that so I'm just going to keep everything just like it is because everything's working." But if you become complacent and don't look after your business, it won't be long before things stop working. If you're not watching your Key Performance Indicators and keeping up with new technology, your competition will overtake you. Complacency is a major pitfall.

I SIGN THE CHECKS, BUT IT'S THE CLIENTS WHO PAY THE SALARIES. I NEVER FORGET THAT.

EGO

This is probably the one I see most. Some lawyers feel like they've achieved real success when they start reading their own press. They think they've got it all figured out. And the truth is, nobody's got it all figured out, ever. I think I know more about marketing than 95 percent of all lawyers, and I still don't have it figured out. It's a moving target and it's always changing. I see lawyers forget where they've come from. They just get fat, dumb, and happy. They become lazy. They fall in love with their law firm and themselves. Let me tell you, that's a surefire way to go under, because you've got to be in love with your clients and your team—not with yourself. It's like I always tell my team members, "I sign the checks, but it's the clients who pay your salaries. Don't you forget that as a lawyer. It's the clients who make all of this possible—not you."

You've done a lot to get where you are, but you should never fall in love with your firm or your business. Be in love with your clients or your customers and your team members, because they are the ones who are going to make the money for you. It's the people—the clients, the staff, the lawyers. It's the people sending you cases, the people who got into a car wreck and then referred you 12 cases over the last 10 years. Those are the people you have to be in love with, because they're the ones who essentially write your paycheck.

DELEGATION

I like to have a well-oiled machine, but there are two things I never delegate: my checkbook and my marketing message. The *way* I implement the message might get delegated, but I'm always in control of the *message* and I'm always in control of my checkbook. I've seen lawyers get sloppy with their checkbooks and let someone else handle them. That is a good way to lose a bunch of money!

You've got to have checks and balances. Smart lawyers get statements sent to their houses and they open them there. You must have someone doing monthly reconciliations. Even if you do all of these things, you can still get burned, but if you do all of these things and let your people know that you're watching, you should be fine. The budget is something you just don't delegate. That's a core belief of mine. I look at the checking balance every morning when I go into my office. That's one of the first things I want to see: how much money I took in yesterday and how much I've got today. Remember, it takes money to build and grow a preeminent law firm.

Of course, the marketing message must also come from you, because it's going to reflect your personality. You can hire people to develop the message but it's got to come from your heart, from your core values. It's got to be you. It's got to be real. If you're not a tough, aggressive lawyer, you don't need to be barking on TV. Just be who you are. There's nothing wrong with being the guy who is easy to talk to.

Robert Kraft from Dallas says, "We're easy to talk to." Plain and simple. He never said he was tough, because he is a nice guy. He probably was pretty tough in court, but that's not the way he portrayed himself. So you've got to have the message that reflects you, the real you. You have to be able to reflect that message and deliver on what you say. Don't delegate that. It's too important to delegate that to someone else.

LOSING FOCUS

Too many times, I see lawyers get lazy about watching their Key Performance Indicators. If you're not inspecting them and measuring them, then your staff's going to quit doing it too, and everybody will become sloppy and lazy. Focus is hard to build, but it's easy to tear down. It's sort of like a reputation. It takes years to build it, but it can be gone in the blink of an eye. One little distraction can send you off in the wrong direction. Maintaining focus is key. I think that goes for any business—not just law firms. It takes time, effort, hard work, intelligence, and action to run a successful business. Never take your success for granted. Never forget where you've come from. And always be willing to change, grow, and learn.

IT'S WHAT YOU LEARN AFTER YOU KNOW IT ALL THAT COUNTS.

I think the legendary baseball manager Earl Weaver said it best when he said, "It's what you learn after you know it all that counts." That was the name of his autobiography and it is a very wise statement. You never stop learning, and you need to instill in yourself and your key management people a desire for continual learning. That means management, that means law, and that means marketing. Because everything is ever changing. The law is ever changing. Marketing is ever changing.

You've got new generations coming up and needing your services. You've got the X and Y and Millennial generations. You have to deal with these people differently than you do with the Baby Boomers. They have different values and they must be handled differently in order to motivate them.

Building a preeminent law firm is not for the meek or the mild, but the rewards can be so great, not just financially but from a personal satisfaction perspective. Being able to build it, systematize it, and grow it to such an extent that you can be proud of it is a great thing. And then you can leave your legacy—something that you can be proud of after you're retired.

For me, it's all about helping people and righting a wrong and getting paid very well to do it. I kill two birds with one stone. I make my clients happy and I make myself happy at the same time.

CONCLUSION

THE SECRET TO GETTING AHEAD
IS GETTING STARTED
—MARK TWAIN

You've just absorbed a great deal of information. You've heard my story, from my beginnings to today. You've learned how I turned my law firm into a preeminent law firm, running at full capacity. You might say, "Man, this is overwhelming. This could take years." Here is my advice to you. Build success in your law firm the same way you would eat an elephant: one bite at a time.

First of all, masterminding is essential. It's one of the keys to my success. I've been either attending or running masterminds for the past 15 years. We need community, and we need to learn from others. Napoleon Hill says it's the number-one lesson for success. I also say if you join an organization like PILMMA, it can be a shortcut to success.

Next, and I cannot say this enough: You need infrastructure, the processes, the procedures, the manuals, the training, and the systems. You have to have your core values and your mission statement. After all of that is in place, then you can start spending money on marketing. You've got to create your message. What's your unique selling proposition (USP)? What's going to make you stand out? Who's your ideal client? What's going to be your message? How are you going to get it to people? Strategically, whom do you want? What is your ideal demographic?

Once you figure all of that out, you can start spending money on a business and marketing plan. Pick one or two marketing tactics and master them, then pick one or two more. As you know, Rome wasn't built in a day. It's a process.

When I come across people who are trying to build a law firm from scratch or trying to turn an existing firm into the preeminent law firm in their market, I tell them to take one step at a time. I tell them to figure out the things I talked about above, and then take one or two tactics and master them.

The first thing I tell people to do is a newsletter. That is an easy first step. Then I tell them to pick another tactic. It might be the Internet; it might be pay-per-click; it might be radio; it might be TV; it might be books. Whatever it is, make sure your message is consistent, and your brand is consistent. Just keep climbing that hill one step at a time and you'll get there. Just keep the faith and know that you're going to meet some obstacles along the way. You're going to have some frustrations along the way. But listen, if it was easy, everybody would be there, right? That's what makes it challenging and exciting.

The biggest problem I see with lawyers is that they procrastinate. Nothing happens until you take action. There's an old proverb that says, "The best time to plant a tree was 20 years ago. When's the second best time? Today." It's like the Nike slogan: "Just do it." You've got to start somewhere.

When I was trying to lose weight, I made all kinds of excuses about why I could start "next week." Well, I never did, so finally I hired a trainer. He said, "No, we're not going to wait. We're going to start today."

YOU CAN'T RIDE A BIKE IF IT'S NOT MOVING.

Whatever it takes to get you from point A to point B, to get you motivated to get it done and to hold you accountable, do it. Whether it is joining a mastermind group, or hiring a coach, a mentor, or a consultant, do it now! Different people need different things to motivate them and get things done, but the big deal, the main message here is, get it and do it. Do it now.

YOUR EXACT NEXT STEPS

First, let me start by congratulating you on how far you have come. You should take a moment to really be proud of yourself because most lawyers never make it even this far. Everyone loves to talk about how they want to grow their practice, make more money and work fewer hours. But few lawyers have the true passion and desire to take action steps to get there.

This book is just step one of the process to turning your hopes and desires into reality. If you allow me, I really want to help you and lead you through the process of getting the practice of your dreams.

There are 2 major steps that will allow me, our staff, and partners to work with you much more closely.

Step #1: Claim your free 2 month Gold trial membership to PILMMA (Personal Injury Lawyers Marketing and Management Association) ($394.00 value)

Please immediately go to www.PILMMA.org/freegift77 and register yourself right away! It's absolutely free and all it takes is an email to register. You not only receive 2 months free membership ($394.00 value) with an additional $432.00 dollars' worth of bonuses:

1. 7 Most Effective Marketing Tactics (CD)
2. Marketing Plan for Lawyers (Product)
3. Why Lawyers Fail to Convert New Callers Into New Clients (Book)
4. Marketing Your Law Firm in the 21st Century (Book)

Step #2 Sign-up and Receive A Digital Download of "A-Z Law Practice Management Blueprint" Workshop (597.00 value)

This one day event completely sold out and is chocked full of forms and processes to effectively hire and manage your staff. Below is just a few of the topics covered.

- **Step-by-Step Checklist for New Hires**
- Creating Job Descriptions
- **Creating an Employee Handbook**
- Establishing Benchmarks
- **How to Create and Utilize an Onboarding Training Manual**
- Productivity Tracking
- **Motivation Techniques**
- Keeping Employee Morale High
- **Creating an Organizational Chart**
- How to Create a Mission Statement
- **How to Interview Applicants Without Getting Fooled**
- How to Deal with Toxic and Problem Employees
- **How to Create a Salary Structure for Staff that Motivates Them to Excel**
- How to Properly Fire an Employee

Just go to www.LawPracticeAdvisor.com/FreeGift22 and commit to three months membership to LawPracticeAdvisor.com for only 37.95 per month. Do yourself a favor and get this invaluable information to boost your income and short-cut your road to success.

This is just the beginning of what we will do for you. My entire team is at your disposal. We are here if you are ready. The rest lies in your hands.

You can start building a life of true financial freedom today. All you need to do is to officially declare it and then follow our programs.